Home Schooling From Scratch

Simple Living — Super Learning

By Mary Potter Kenyon

Gazelle Publications

Gazelle Publications

Excellence in education since 1976

Transition address:
9853 Jericho Rd., Bridgman, MI 49106
wadeted@aol.com
For sales, or address after 2/97: (800) 650-5076

Text by Mary Potter Kenyon
Copyright © 1996

Line drawings for chapters by Lishi Laurance
Copyright © 1996

All rights reserved

ISBN: 0-930192-35-4
LC Catalog Card No: 95-81888

Contents

This book is dedicated ...

❋ To my dear husband David, who has spent his share of time at the park with our youngest children so I could write, and who has been my biggest supporter.

❋ To my Mother, Irma Potter, who has been instrumental in my choices to home school and write and who was an exemplary role model for a fledgling penny pincher.

❋ To my good friend Mary Humston who has encouraged my writing since the beginning, and

❋ To my brother Lyle, whose only payment for a gift of a computer has been my undying gratitude, and now mention in this book.

My thanks ...

to the following home schoolers who took the time to fill out my questionnaire. Ideas attributed to these people will list their initials and home states.

Sarah Acker, Jackson, Mississippi
Carol Anderson, Columbus, Ohio
Rhonda Barfield,
   St. Charles, Missouri
Valerie Berg, Boulder, Colorado
Renée Bjork, Belgrade, Minnesota
Laua Buffi, El Sabrante, California
Joceyln Butler,
   Chocowinity, North Carolina
Carol Burris, Miramar, Florida
Janine Calsbeek, Orange City, Iowa
Valerie Close, Independence, Iowa
Marion Cohen, Philadelphia, Pennsylvania
Laurie Colecchi, Akron, Ohio
Marjorie Crandall, Thornton, Colorado
Therese Cravins,
   La Crosse, Wisconsin
Susan Dahlem, Many, Louisiana
Cherylee Duncan, Brookline, Missouri
Terri Earl, Grass Valley, Oregon
Nancy Eason, Fort Collins, Colorado
Beth Garcia, Enfield, Connecticut
Judy Gormley, Vallejo, California
Helen Hegener, Tonasket, Washington
Sue Hodgson, St. Louis, Missouri
Katie Jackman, Ames, Iowa
Neysa Jensen, Boise, Idaho

Marisa Lapish, Madison, Ohio
Kathy Littman, Santa Rosa, California
Gina Merrick, St. Charles, Missouri
Shelley Noonan, Humphrey, Nebraska
Elizabeth Perkins,
   Florissant, Missouri
Lou Anna Perkins, Penobscot, Maine
Debbie Pitrone, Akron, Ohio
Marsha Ransom,
   South Haven, Michigan
Linda and Bob Schneider,
   Cambridge, Illinois
Maria Smith, Kempton, Pennsylvania
Sandra Spangler, Berea, Ohio
Terry Steinmetz,
   Bark River, Michigan
Kim Stewart, Independence, Iowa
Denise Suarez, Healdsburg, California
Patricia Townsend,
   Blowing Rock, North Carolina
Margaret Turano, Davis, California
Suzanne Wagner,
   Fairfield, Connecticut
Sandy Ward, Elkton, Maryland
Jane Wood, Aurora, Illinois
Norma Young,
   Pennsburg, Pennsylvania

❄

Two words from the publisher

Although this book is not about religion, Mary's confidence in God is evident. May I share a brief comment, too? My wife, Karen, and I have committed a tenth of our income for God's work. It isn't that He is dependent on us but that He has given us the opportunity, as very minor partners, to help bring His love to this hateful world. Setting aside the ten percent (and more) before any other consideration, helps us remember that He will take care of the rest. Over the years, as we have *put God first*, He has honored His promise (Mal. 3:10, 11) in abundant blessings, not measurable in dollars.

Now let's talk about a second principle in harmony with what you will read in this book: *Dream dreams but remember reality.* Too many people only dream. Insecurity begs them for money to relieve anxieties while the troubles only pile up. We must learn to recognize rationalization and to say no to foolish expenditures. We must make a budget, avoid borrowing if possible, and refuse to spend a penny unless it's left over after we have accounted for commitments and necessities, and if a reserve is available for emergencies. Then we can relax and enjoy the simple things as Mary suggests.

Likely you already understand all this. I just want to remind you (and myself) that, *by chasing the happiness of wealth, we will miss the wealth of real happiness.*

Ted Wade

1 My journey into home schooling

That was it! We were going to home school. My son Michael had just become a junior kindergarten dropout – or I could say, "takeout." As a college student I had written several papers on home schooling and believed it to be a valid option for many parents – for many, but probably not for me. My major wasn't education, and at that time, home schooling in Iowa without a teaching certificate was illegal anyway.

Years later, with the third of my four children poised to enter the public school system, I was ready to learn more about home schooling. Already somewhat dissatisfied with the school system, I had volunteered to interview a local home schooling couple for a feature in our local newspaper. These parents were spending over $300 per child, per year, on their home schooling system, and the interview left me feeling a little disappointed, more sure than ever that my family couldn't do it. There was just no way our single income from my husband's social-work job would make home schooling a feasible option.

"As iron sharpens iron, so one man sharpens another." Proverbs 27:17, NIV.

But now Michael's needs had leaped to top priority, and I opened the door to meet the challenge.

Parents choose home schooling for many reasons. My own early schooling exposure began at the premature age of four when I became a not-so-eager participant in the pilot program for Project Head Start in Dubuque, Iowa. I vividly remember holding back tears during the entire half-day program, enjoying only the midmorning snack and the array of toys. Although some would cite this early exposure to school as instrumental in my future educational aspirations, I expect that my next year skipping kindergarten and the thirty-six consecutive days I missed in the third grade had much more to do with my natural zest for learning. In reality, I was a closet home schooler, learning to read and to search for knowledge at the feet of loving parents. School was merely a tolerated vehicle for knowledge. My cherished school learning took place from my lap under the crude wooden desks of my elementary classrooms where I read and re-read favorite books while my classmates plodded along in their readers.

I went on to graduate from college because I continued to love learning. My husband is well aware that if we ever get rich, I'll take classes just for fun. I fully expected my children to have the same zest for learning, but unfortunately, I saw that spark dim in my older two children the farther along they got in school. Their creativity and their natural interests were squelched in a classroom setting of peers where they were expected to conform to a set way of thinking. Worksheets and books that were brought home reflected the mentality of a world that my husband and I found offensive. The children liked school. They had no problems adjusting to being away from home. That is, until Michael.

We had started Michael in a half-day junior kindergarten at age five because we realized the all-day Kindergarten might be too much for him. He was a homebody, loving to spend all day playing with his little sister. Although I still contemplated home schooling at times, I was expecting our fifth child and had many reasons for sticking with the traditional school system. Michael's negative experience with that system finally prompted more research. He began having headaches and stomachaches, wouldn't eat breakfast, and cried when the bus came to pick him up. He also started hitting his little sister when he was home. When his teacher told me he'd adjusted fine and was participating in the fighting and shoving on the playground, the die was cast for school at home! I pulled him out of junior kindergarten midyear and began earnestly researching ways to teach him myself. His older sister, Beth, joined us at home at the sixth-grade level.

My decision to home school was not made simply on the basis of Michael's immaturity that year. His experience only exacerbated a dissatisfaction with the school system that I'd probably harbored since my own childhood.

My first obstacle when deciding to home school was financial. How could I possibly afford it? This book stems from that concern.

While the consumer marketplace is saturated with newsletters and books for self-avowed tightwads and frugal shoppers, I have found none specifically for the home schooler. Yet we, more often than most families, must live on one income. Many of the books I read helped me get started and formulate plans for that first year, but none addressed the subject of home schooling on a budget.

I was used to saving money. I grew up in a household where making do was the rule. My mother could make something out of nothing and was a wonderful example for me. Although not as adept as she at working from scratch, saving money on clothing and feeding a family of seven was second nature to me. Hitting garage sales in the early morning, scouting the clearance aisles and collecting cents-off coupons at the local recycling center were just a few of the ways I'd found to economize. Locally, I was known as a coupon queen for my grocery store savings. I even appeared in a Joan Lunden video on couponing distributed to doctor's offices. So, with our home schooling, I naturally began looking for ways to save money.

Initially, I sold a camcorder I'd gotten free through refunding. I used the $350 for periodical subscriptions, the purchase of textbooks for two students, and for an afternoon in a school supply store where I indulged in a dozen workbooks, paper, clay and a variety of pencils. The purchases seemed wise, but I will never again spend that much in a single home schooling year unless I want to.

From personal experience, and by communicating with other frugal parents, I have found many ways home schoolers can save money. In these pages you will discover a compendium of ideas and a listing of helpful resources. You can acquire the books and supplies you need without the threat of bankruptcy. Home schooling does not have to be an expensive endeavor. Through my questionnaires, I have met families who spend as little as $30 per year and families who spend as much as $3000. The amounts spent were relative; each home teacher felt they were saving money.

If you are new to home schooling, relax. You don't have to spend vast amounts of money to ensure that your children receive a good education. If you've been home schooling for years, you will likely still find new ways to conserve your resources. Other people's successful experiences can guide you. All the families I've met through ads in various home schooling publications had one thing in common – creative ideas. While at no time do I recommend being "cheap" with your child's future, it only makes sense to stretch your education dollars. About using coupons, someone once commented, "It's just pennies," and I replied, "Yes, but I regularly save 3000 of those pennies at the grocery store each week." The same goes for home schooling. Make your pennies count.

2 Deciding how to teach them

> "*The homeschool community has created a huge market and industry around itself. We're in a buyer's market and that is, in many ways, good. But a lot of people are being intimidated and the intimidation is hurtful. My concern or fear is that there is a lot of guilt, a lot of expectations put on the average family that the Lord didn't put there. Families certainly didn't spend $5,000 a year in Old Testament times and we don't need to now. . . . Poorer families are very often the best homeschoolers. They're more resourceful, simplistic, common sense oriented.*" *Workshop presenter Carole Seid, in an interview with editor Shari Henry,* Heart of Homeschooling, *May 1995.*

I remember the wonder in the eyes of my fifteen-month-old as snowflakes drifted down from the sky. His awe at the sight of God's creation is akin to my own feeling as I watch my children learn. What a privilege to be a part of the process! I have watched understanding dawn when my first grader realized he could read a sentence on his own. And I have felt satisfaction from my oldest daughter's reading interests and ability. No PTA committee I could join at a school, and no amount of volunteer work would ever bring the same quality of involvement with my children's education. To me, home schooling is a challenge and a delight. I find myself learning along with my oldest daughter. I am relearning facts and figures I had once memorized and promptly forgot after a test. I continually search for ways to make the information a little more interesting and pertinent, so she won't forget.

Your definition of home schooling

What does home schooling mean to you? Do you simply expect school at home? Do you have educational goals for your children? Do you believe there are certain things children should learn at particular ages? If you haven't already asked yourself these questions, ask them now. Take time to write down general and specific goals for your children's education. Then re-define them as you learn more about your children. Most long-time home schoolers have very definite ideas on how and what they want their children to learn.

If, like me, you have taken a child out of a school setting, both you and your child may have to "de-school." I use this term in a general sense, not quite aligning myself with those who subscribe to John Holt's unschooling approach. In my case, de-schooling meant learning that our home program did not have to be a copy of the public school classroom schedule, nor did we have to follow the strict regimen of the parochial school she had once attended.

My fear of failing to cover large blocks of important learning was largely unfounded according to the testimony of unschoolers I have corresponded with. While textbooks are almost essential for such subjects as calculus and geometry, there is much to be said for using beautifully illustrated "real" books for at least some of your lessons on history and science. While there are many wonderful textbooks on the market, children can learn a great deal from books such as biographies of famous people, stories from a specific time period of history, or nonfiction books related to their specific interests. They might enjoy the reading so much that they don't even realize they are learning!

Through the diverse group of parents participating in my project, I was able to renew my own convictions about home learning. Precisely because of this flexibility and diversity, home teaching methods can be adapted to fit different kinds of families.

> I think the point has to be made that there is no way that any curriculum can meet the needs of all children. The beauty of home schooling is that every parent and child can work out a tailor-made program that suits their needs and interests. It's as simple as that. –Micki Colfax, co-author of *Home schooling For Excellence* in *Home Education Magazine*, March/April, 1991. Used by permission.

Ruth Beechick agrees that no one way of home schooling is just right for every family. In her book, *You Can Teach Your Child Successfully*, she writes: "You parents naturally know how to relate to each of your children and to help them learn. Your biggest problem is that so many of you are afraid that teachers or society or somebody out there will frown on your way of teaching. You feel safer if you stick closely to a book or series of books, because that is somebody else's plan, that is in print, that must be right.

"For some children and for some of the time, certain books will happen to be just right. But if you find yourself struggling to mold your child to a book, try reversing priorities. It's the child you are teaching, not the book. Bend

the book, or find another; make the studies fit the child."
(Used by permission.)

I know parents who plan their daily teaching much as
regular schools do with specific time periods for each subject. This is okay, if it works for them. Many families allow
for a more flexible schedule, and some seem to work best
with little scheduling at all! I love Donn Reed's honest ac-
count in his *Home School Source Book* of his family's search for
a method and style of home schooling that would work for
their lifestyle. Textbooks? No textbooks? Schedules? No
schedules? The Reeds struggle to find what worked for them
is a real–life example of how flexible home schooling can be.
Flexibility makes it easier to save money.

Choosing a curriculum approach

Families who enroll their child in an accredited program
through a satellite or umbrella school may pay more than
$300.00 a year, per child. This fee may cover textbooks as
well as homework instructions, testing services, and phone
consultation. They have the security of a well-formulated
plan, albeit someone else's plan.

Some parents who would like this type of structured
program are unable to pay the tuition. Others who could
afford it find it too much like the school environment they
are trying to escape. "If we were going to use school-type
programs, we'd send the kids to school," writes Jocelyn Butler.

There are other options. If you like the security of a series of books from an umbrella school, consider purchasing
only their materials. Most teacher's manuals contain sample
daily plans. Kim Stewart, a certified teacher and home
schools consultant suggests taking the number of pages in
the textbooks and figure roughly how many pages would
need to be covered for each of the three-month periods.
Daily schedules may be planned from that estimate.

The unit studies method of home schooling allows for a structured flexibility. A unit can draw on a particular time period or other area of interest incorporating history, science, language, and writing through extensive research. For parents who don't feel comfortable designing their own unit studies, several people, including Valerie Bendt have prepared outlines with lists of books on certain topics. A decided advantage of unit study is that one book or one series of books can serve the entire family for a subject or for a block of time.

Another instructional option is to design your own curriculum. You can incorporate books and other materials you have on hand, while planning extensive use of the library's free resources. This option costs less, assuming you already have suitable resources. And, if you don't, you can often

---

Just as structure in a curriculum may have undesirable effects, so can moving away from structure into projects or study areas dictated largely by current interests. Of course children and families differ and should not be expected to fit the same pattern. But that fact is not justification for a lack of using good books, and planning carefully.

Be sure to keep the future doors of learning open for your kids. For this, they need (1) a large base of information about the world they live in, although a few minor gaps are no problem, (2) solid skills in areas including language and mathematics, and (3) habits of serious, focused study, even with the more tedious learning tasks. Unit studies, as often advocated, increase the risk of weakness in these three areas. By careful planning you can have the advantages of both structure and creative freedom.

–Ted Wade, author of *The Home School Manual.*

**Curriculum Options
From More to Less Expensive**

♦ Use full guidance sources and materials from a home schooling provider

♦ Use only the materials and curriculum guide from a provider

♦ Use selected textbooks and supplemental reading, plan your own curriculum around them, possibly with the help of a professional teacher

♦ Follow unit studies along with selected textbooks

---

buy secondhand texts and materials through businesses listed in the resource chapter.

Modifying your program

At least twice a year, you will want to evaluate objectives and methods. Scan catalogs and check out inexpensive ways to add good materials. Summer months are ideal for this planning, but whenever you find that something is not working for your family, take the time to seriously reconsider methods and materials. Simply changing books might be all you need to keep the educational gears running smoothly. When my first-grader became bored and frustrated with a complex phonics set complete with flash cards, blend charts, and writing pages, I found that substituting a simpler single book gave him the confidence he needed.

The elaborate phonics set could have cost me over $100. I'm glad I bought it second-hand. I order materials through used book suppliers several times a year, and through other suppliers when discounts are steep enough to warrant my attention. Buying materials secondhand helps cut my financial loss if they don't prove useful. When I resell them, I get closer to what I paid.

To preview what you might like to use, check out curriculum fairs or plan a materials "show and tell" at support group meetings. And remember that no matter how highly recommended something is, if it doesn't meet your family's needs it's a bad investment. To reiterate Ruth Beechick's advice, plan the curriculum around your child, not the other way around. The flexibility inherent in home schooling is to your advantage in saving money.

Books, books, books . . . and supplies

The first time I took my children to the library thirty-five miles away, my six-year-old Michael got out of the car and stood in awe in front of the huge building. I literally saw goose bumps rise on his arms. "I'm so excited, I'm shivering," he exclaimed in wonder.

That's the way I feel about books. Books excite me. Books on sale excite me even more. As a child, I thought only rich people owned an abundance of books. Images of walls of books on television programs represented true wealth to me then, and I feel very rich now with my shelves full of books.

> "The man who does not read good books has no advantage over the man who can't read them."
>
> – Mark Twain

I was a voracious reader growing up. My two younger sisters and I would often trek to the library on a Friday night, each checking out four or five books. By Sunday afternoon we'd be trading books, having finished those we'd checked out for ourselves!

Using the library

There's a consensus among thrifty home schoolers that their most prized possession is their library card. Many who answered my questionnaire use the library as their primary source of home schooling materials. For one family, it was the only source.

As you use the library, teach your older children basic library skills. They should understand the Dewey Decimal system, methods of research, use of the cataloging system, how to make bibliography cards, and how to find what they want in *The Reader's Guide to Periodical Literature* and other reference books.

Also help your children learn the art of choosing good literature. Review reading lists with them. The Christian Life Workshop offers a free list suggesting classical works as well as more recent ones they consider acceptable. (See the resource chapter.) You probably have a list of your own favorites from childhood that you would like to enjoy again with your children. Even young children can learn to locate books by the author's last name as soon as they are familiar

---

Skills to teach at the library

◆ The Dewey Decimal System

◆ Alphabetical order

◆ The use of reference books

◆ The use of resources available by computer

◆ The use of the card catalogue, now often on computer

◆ Research methods, involving bibliography cards and outlines

The Dewey Decimal System

This is the classification system still used in US public libraries. University libraries use the Library of Congress System. Each of the hundred-number units is further subdivided. The library catalog card number indicates where the book is located. In the same shelf location other books related to the topic may be found.

000-099	General works
100-199	Philosophy and psychology
200-299	Religion
300-399	Social science
400-499	Language
500-599	Science
600-699	Technology
700-799	Arts: fine arts and crafts
800-899	Literature
900-999	History, geography, travel, biography

with the alphabetical order.

Unit Studies make good use of the library. Rhonda Barfield and her four children use the library to find books and videos for their unit studies. They order them through inter–library loan if necessary.

Gina Merrick uses library books such as those in the Little House series for unit studies. She and her children read the books, act out parts from the story, and even make costumes and cook recipes from them. This way reading, drama, and home economics are all studied using a single book!

When the Suarez family studied the period of history between 1840 and 1860, their research at the library covered political and government factions, current events, important people, social customs and values, diet, geographical regions, transportation, and so on. Subtopics included clothing, and traditions.

Utilize your public library to the fullest: Check out educational videos, borrow on inter-library loan, check out art prints, and attend story times if your younger children are interested. "Wear out your library card," advises Jocelyn Butler.

Building a home resource center

A personal home library is as important as access to a public library. Some home schoolers are so surrounded by books that their children seem to simply absorb the knowledge in them! Helen and Mark Hegener, publishers of *Home Education Magazine*, own thousands of books on the many subjects that interest their family of seven. While the majority of their home library comes from used book sales, garage sales and library sales, they always give quality, expensive books for Christmas and birthday.

A home schooling acquaintance surprised me with the comment, "Wow, you have a lot of books. We don't buy books. They cost too much." But do they? Mary Pride cites her willingness to purchase many good, Christian books as a key factor in her becoming an author. In her words,

---

Benefits of a home library

"Books in the home provide children with extraordinary benefits. They have immediate access to good literature, resource materials, vocabulary sources, reference information, pictures, photographs and more. All this helps turn nonreaders into readers and readers into writers."

— Jane Williams, in *How to Stock a Home Library Inexpensively*, Third Edition (used by permission).

"Wisdom is your very best investment and whatever helps you get wiser is the best investment of your time and money." (*All the Way Home*, page 136.)

Building up your home library isn't difficult, and it doesn't need to cost a tremendous amount either. Basic research tools such as a dictionary, an atlas, and perhaps a thesaurus, should be available to your children at home. A good encyclopedia set is also important, but can be costly. To avoid the expense, use the sets at your public library.

I have found garage sales to be a wonderful source for good books. While you might hit several garage sales in a row where only Harlequin romances are considered good reading, I have found used readers for a quarter, and entire boxes of old books for only a dollar or two. I have also discovered workbooks with only a few pencil marks! My favorite buys have been books I read and loved as a child.

Another good source for used books is library book sales. Several libraries within thirty-five miles of us have annual sales. These are gold mines. You may need to spend an hour or two sifting through tons of books which, of course, is a book lover's dream! A recent library book sale netted me 18 history magazines, 6 children's books, and a dozen adult books for less than $14! One of these books was new and would have cost me $12 at the bookstore.

There is usually no room for a baby or toddler among the stacks or shelves of books, but your older children can help scout out the good books. If your local library doesn't already have an annual book sale, see if you can get one started! Libraries generally have a friends-of-the-library volunteer group that appreciates ideas for fund raisers.

You can also find treasures at used bookstores. Check the yellow pages for a store near you. If you are looking for a specific title or topic the proprietor may be able to help you. Our bookstore, *Once Upon a Time Family Books*, specializes in the old classics, pre-1960 juvenile literature series, and other books for home schooling or Christian families.

Estate auctions can yield exciting treasures for book lovers who don't mind waiting for the auctioneers to reach the boxes of books amongst the other items to be auctioned. A recent auction netted my husband and me a hayrack full of boxes of books for $1. Even though we donated more than half the books, we still uncovered an original McGuffey's reader and Ray's arithmetic, as well as dozens of books to shelve in our store.

Some businesses specialize in used school books. This category includes small mail-order businesses operated by home schoolers themselves. Bob and Linda Schneider, for example, operate the Rainbow Resource Center. They sell used textbooks on a consignment basis through an inventoried catalog. Similar businesses have sprung up to fill the need of home schoolers who like to save money by purchasing second-hand materials.

Where to find books

- ◆ Mail-order book sellers
- ◆ Book clubs
- ◆ Second-hand sources
    mail order
    special bookstores
- ◆ Garage sales
- ◆ Thrift stores
- ◆ Discount stores
- ◆ Library sales

A great way to buy discounted paperback books is through book clubs that mail catalogs to public school classrooms. Get on their mailing list for yourself or request catalogs for your entire home schooling support group. Scholastic Book Clubs recently offered an unedited paperback of *Little Women* for only $2.95 and the entire set of C. S. Lewis books for $12.95 (a $40 value!). What's more, these clubs offer free books with minimum orders. Catalogs from Trumpet and Golden Book feature items for purchase by teachers. I have ordered number and letter rubber stamps and other educational aids unavailable at stores near me. Addresses for these clubs are listed in the resource chapter. Make sure to mention what grades you teach when you ask for catalogs.

For additional inexpensive reading material , subscribe to the *Weekly Reader* or a similar classroom periodical for each grade level you teach. For around $7 a year your child can get a weekly news magazine and a monthly educational poster. Christian school magazines include *God's World* and *Discovery* (800) 234–8558.

Book clubs advertise in just about every magazine you read. They offer three to five books at very low introductory prices and your promise to buy an additional one to four books within a certain time. Depending on the club's offerings and on what you really need, this initial purchase could save you a good deal of money. Even with the inevitably high shipping charges and subsequent required purchases, I have gotten some excellent resources for our schooling at an average cost of only four or five dollars per book, instead of fifteen to twenty–five. I usually buy the additional required books for Christmas or a birthday and then cancel my membership. The only club I have found beneficial enough for our family to continue membership in is the Conservative Book Club. Besides their wonderful array of conservative best sellers, they offer many books specifically for home schoolers. The Homeschooling Book Club is another excellent source for good books, and they require no minimum purchase!

A number of mail order suppliers offer materials for home teaching at drastic discounts. Order several catalogs and compare prices.

At a University bookstore you can find good educational materials, particularly for your high schooler. Often these stores will offer out–of–print or no–longer–used textbooks at big discounts. Ask when they have sales scheduled. Who says high school students must learn only from high school textbooks? If your child is interested in learning about psychology, sociology or anthropology, for example, a textbook from an introductory college course could be ideal. Watch for humanistic influences in social science books and evolution in science books. Help your youth become a discerning reader. At a nearby university bookstore, I've gotten textbooks for as little as $1, and general interest books for a quarter, sometimes only a black marker line across the page edges indicating it a sale book. Prices drop for old editions.

Of course, for some books you are willing to pay full price. My family loves the books put out by Klutz Press including *Explorabook*, a book full of science experiments including everything you need to conduct them. Klutz publishes similar books on juggling, bug-watching, and hair-braiding . Our family loves the Dorling-Kindersley books so much that we were tempted to become distributors for them! Their popular *Eyewitness* science series includes excellent learning tools. Look for books like these at discount stores and on sale shelves at bookstores. I have seen well-worn display copies of some of these books in clearance aisles for half the original price. Make bookstore browsing a family event.

Your children may find it fun to trade inexpensive paper-backs through the mail with a pen pal. My daughter keeps a brown paper sack next to her bed for books she doesn't want to keep. She either shares them or sells them at a our bookstore. She has learned to be a very discerning reader and recognizes "classic" books she will want to share with her children or to re-read on a cold winter's day.

School supplies

What about school supplies to go along with the books you buy? Most home schoolers who answered my question-naire shopped the before-school sales every fall. I suggest checking the school supply aisles a week or two *after* school resumes. You may find erasers, pencil sharpeners, crayons, pens, pencils and writing tablets even cheaper.

Many mail-order businesses cater to the special needs of home schoolers, offering blank books, science equipment, or other supplies otherwise hard to locate. Terry Steinmetz saves money on science equipment such as petri dishes and test tubes by combining orders with other families to a

supply company to get a cheaper quantity price. Tree-Top Publishing offers a variety of blank books for school projects.

School supply stores are also great places to get clay, pastels and educational games but the prices are hefty. Get on their mailing lists for advance notice of clearance sales. I have bought huge packages of art paper discounted to half-price simply because their outside wrappers were torn. Valerie Close,sends for the catalogs to get ideas for making homemade games or flash cards.

Award certificates and stickers are, of course, optional but fun to use and generally not too expensive. School supply stores sell these, as do home school supply catalogs. You may be lucky enough to spot some of these supplemental items at garage sales or thrift stores. I still have reward stickers I bought at a retired teacher's sale several years ago.

We have also found maps, a globe, alphabet charts, an abacus, and a three-hole punch at garage sales. National Geographic publishes wonderful maps. We have purchased an entire box full of the magazines at a yard sale for $1 just for the maps! None of these items is a necessity but if you have any visual learners in your family, they can be especially helpful.

Computer supplies, and even a computer itself can add to your home learning. I am blessed to have a computer, but only because of a very generous brother who gave me his two-year-old Packard Bell. We could never have afforded even an older model. I am surprised to find more and more home schoolers who have "inherited" an older computer or purchased one at a sale. This might be an item worth begging for! One mother who answered my questionnaire was given a computer by someone in her support group who wanted to upgrade. Her family was definitely satisfied with what they could still do with the older model. While a computer isn't essential for a home school, it is a valuable tool! If you are worried about your children's computer literacy, check your library. Many have a computer the public can use. You can learn the basics right along with your children from a helpful staff person. Your high school student may want to sign up for adult education classes on computer skills.

Three companies in the resource section offer computer software at low prices. Keep in mind, however, when the software is marketed as shareware, you will be asked to send an additional fee to the author of the program if you choose to continue using it. You can find inexpensive software in local stores, too. I have even seen cute educational programs for as low as $7.99 at toy stores! Check the system requirements shown on the package to be sure the program will work on your older computer.

Buy an old typewriter at a garage sale for your younger students to learn basic keyboard skills. All my children have fun "writing" stories on the typewriter, and my daughter Rachel practically learned the alphabet by banging away on the typewriter and looking at our wall alphabet chart.

Whatever supplies you buy, you will want to manage them in an organized way. Organization techniques will be discussed in Chapter Seven.

4 Beg, borrow, and barter

People interested in my children's education have given me magazines, books, and file folders of information. Once you inform friends and family about home schooling, their generosity will surprise you. Even strangers might contribute to your educational endeavors as Laura Buffi found out when she asked a retail store for old fabric sample books. When the owner discovered Laura wanted them for home schooling art projects, she added party invitation books and rug samples. Laura also befriended school teachers who tended to throw out leftover supplies once or twice a year.

Though I draw the line at regular dumpster diving as a family field trip, I have been known to pull particularly interesting items from the curbside trash. I've found rolls of Christmas wrap, wallpaper sample books and boxes of magazines. Marion Cohen has retrieved treasure troves of books in this way! I am not suggesting you don Halloween masks and rubber gloves to search the streets for enticing dumpsters and garbage piles. I am merely pointing out how a resourceful parent watches for opportunities.

Ask your local librarian what they do with old magazines and offer to carry them off for posters, murals, and recipe collections. When word gets out that your family accepts boxes of unwanted *National Geographic* magazines, you may experience more generosity than you can handle!

If relatives ask, suggest educational games and books as Christmas or birthday gifts. Isn't there a science kit or a juggling book you and your children would dearly love but don't dare spend the money on? You might rationalize your purchase as a gift, like Helen Hegener does, or you could supply generous relatives with a favorite catalog or two!

Check classified ads offering items for the carting away. I have seen ads for swing sets (for physical education), barn boards (for painting classes), and sandboxes free for the taking. Consider running an ad of your own, asking for the types of items you could use.

An area university extension office may offer free information you can use for home learning. Do you want to teach your teenager to can tomatoes? Would you like information on raising sheep? Would you like a food groups chart for your health class? The extension office is likely to have pamphlets on everything from babies to zippers!

Many government and private agencies will send you free posters, magnets, bookmarks or pamphlets on subjects you can study. You can pay for books or magazines that list these freebies or check your local library for the same information. Just remember to keep an eye on your educational goals so that California prunes don't crowd the principles of evaporation and sublimation out of your science program.

Sandy Ward used to send for all the free offers she could until she realized that many of the materials were just cluttering her files and not being used for learning. "I'm starting to be choosier, and have learned that free isn't necessarily good," she wrote. Use common sense before wasting a stamp. Will you use that pamphlet on baking-soda crafts? Do you really need a poster on cotton production? Naturally, if your son or daughter has developed an interest in stamp collecting, it would be worth your while to order a booklet on the topic. Or if you just like receiving mail, you can send for every offer that even remotely interests someone in your family.

Develop your youngster's writing ability by having them write out the requests and address the envelopes.

Borrowing things

Should "begging" not appeal to you, try borrowing. A museum near us offers classes on the use of microscopes and then loans the instruments for several days at a time to graduates of the course, usually public school teachers. You could ask about similar opportunities in your area. Libraries often lend video and audio tapes and even art prints which can become a part of your lessons. See if the video center in your community has educational titles. (Finding them may remind you of dumpster diving.)

Some home schooling support groups sponsor a lending library. Make your needs known. Someone in your group may be willing to loan their materials or equipment for a few days or weeks. Or you could advertise in a local newsletter to borrow items you are looking for. A microscope, a pottery wheel, and a sewing machine are examples of items I would like access to for my own children's learning.

Borrowing talent—apprenticeships

In an apprenticeship type of arrangement, a person trades work for knowledge and expertise. It's like borrowing them. The apprenticeship is one of the oldest and most successful methods of learning a marketable skill. For at least 600 years, apprentices have learned their crafts under contract with employers. The arrangement requires the employer provide instruction in exchange for a specified time of service. The training is mutually beneficial.

Although apprenticeships may be connected with a high school core curriculum, they are the main post elementary education for some youth. *Growing Without Schooling* magazine abounds with stories of teenagers who have been apprenticed with older, more knowledgeable adults in their fields of interest and who have developed successful careers. Reuben, son of LouAnna Perkins, became an apprentice at a local bakery and found customers who were eager to hire such an industrious young man for other jobs.

Of course many careers such as medicine, law, and science require a more formal education. For general purposes, however, apprenticeships can be a loosely based method for your home schooler to have hands-on experience in areas of interest. And learning a trade is a good idea for professional people.

If your daughter is interested in being a vet, ask your local vet if there is any volunteer work she could do once or twice a week. Real-life experience might change her vocational goals, or reinforce them.

Apprenticeships
As the term is traditionally understood

▼   Are practical learning programs of structured, systematic, on-the-job training. These programs are clearly defined and commonly recognized throughout an industry.

▼   Involve manual, mechanical, and/or technical skills and knowledge acquired during a minimum of 2,000 hours of experience in the particular type of job.

▼   Include related instruction to supplement on-the-job training.

From information in *Guide to Apprenticeship Programs*, by William Shanahan, Arco, 1983.

When my daughter's interests turned to retail sales, she worked with my sister in her consignment store for two afternoons and loved it. Baby sitting jobs sparked her interest in working with children, so she offered her services to a nearby preschool. When she turns 14, she will be eligible to participate in a program to help teens learn about police work.

The US Department of Labor's Bureau of Apprenticeship and Training lists over 830 apprenticeable occupations as alternatives to college for young people. A certificate of completion is offered after a two to four year training program. Check your local library or employment office for information about government sponsored programs. Some 1500 programs in more than 76 categories are listed in a two-volume guide from J. G. Ferguson.

The *Mentor Apprenticeship Exchange* is a newsletter and directory which helps connect people in the US and Canada who have something to teach with people who want to learn. (See the resources chapter.)

Bartering

Do you have an excess of produce from your garden, an attic full of maternity or baby clothes you'll never use again, or even a skill or talent you could share that would be valuable to someone else? If you can cut hair or hem dresses, you have a skill that others might not have and would be willing to barter for. Bartering has been around for a long time and is simply trading one skill or product for another of like value. With ten children in my family, I started bartering at a young age. My sisters and I traded everything from clothing to hair ribbons. Now my husband and I use a barter system whenever we can. When we couldn't afford a station wagon we had our heart set on, we bartered an extra television and partial cash payment to buy it. Terry Steinmetz swapped her baked goods for piano lessons for her children.

You can trade through a well-organized newsletter like The *Christian Home School Swapletter*. I have traded magazines for magazines, books for books, and even excess toiletries I'd gotten through double couponing for diapers, books and clothing.

In the US, don't forget the government when bartering is part of your income. The IRS taxes bartering that becomes part of your gross income. Don't worry too much, however. These laws hardly apply to trading your children's T-shirts and tennis shoes with the woman down the street. Consult a tax professional if you have a question.

If your support group is interested in a unique activity, try organizing a special swap meet, where mothers can bring their extra curriculum materials, toys, educational games, or even clothes, and trade for items of like value. People can assign their own values for items they bring. My older sister used to trade unwanted children's clothing, magazines, or household items with other housewives each month, calling the event a "dust-catcher's party." I've recently revived that practice with a couple of my sisters at my mother's house on Friday afternoons.

Stretch your imagination when searching for ways to use what you have to get what you need.

5 Where to find support

Following my decision to home school, I faced the same question from well-meaning friends and relatives as when I was pregnant with our fifth child: "Are you sure you know what you're doing?" Fortunately, I had a mother and husband who strongly supported my decision, but it would have been nice to have known another home schooler, an old pro who could take me under her wing and share her tribulations and triumphs. Home schooling support groups are invaluable for this kind of help.

Support groups

As a new home schooler, I was eager to join a support group. I needed the encouragement, and I thought my children needed the socialization. My first experience was greatly disappointing. Most of the members attended the same church and home schooled in a very structured manner. After several meetings I realized that no one who departed from a set curriculum in any way would feel welcome. The meetings left me feeling more lonely than before, so I stopped going.

From the responses I received for this book, many home school support groups truly do encourage different approaches to home schooling and serve as a network for parents who have made home education a top priority. A good support group could reassure couples struggling to make ends meet by providing opportunities to make friends with people who have succeeded in pulling the ends together. Support groups can also organize inexpensive activities and field trips for families and set up curriculum fairs and old-fashioned swap meets. The support group Terry Steinmetz attends sponsors a curriculum fair each year where members may buy, sell, or trade. Joceyln Butler's North Carolina support group gets together for "cultural dinners" where families bring artifacts, books or music from the culture being studied. Often ethnic costumes are worn. The group has even had speakers, dancers and storytellers representing the different cultures. Other support groups have a lending library, saving money for members who can't afford to invest in many good home schooling books. The possibilities are practically endless!

Other groups

Groups outside of home schooling also provide socialization opportunities. You may find or establish a group for children with like interests. 4-H groups were the top choice for the home schoolers I corresponded with, followed closely by church youth groups. Other home schooled children participated in city sports teams, dancing classes, horse training, and various clubs that supported their interests, if not their method of schooling. You don't necessarily have to join groups to participate in their activities. Some home schoolers attend college art fairs, concerts, or presentations and speeches. Others participate in county fair exhibits. And some even receive permission from area schools to participate in class field trips.

Newsletters and magazines

Where a support group doesn't exist or fails to meet your needs, a good newsletter or magazine can help. I eagerly await each issue of a favorite magazine just so I can reaffirm my choices in schooling. I receive several other magazines as well and usually send for samples of new magazines or newsletters for home schoolers. Plenty of such periodicals exist so most families can find one they like. You could go broke subscribing to them all, so send for samples to find ones that serve your family best.

The magazines I get are chock–full of ideas, tips, hints, stories from other home schoolers, and articles that affirm our choices to be home schoolers even during the tough times. In fact, several well–written articles encouraged me to continue home schooling during a particularly adverse time in our life. I had given birth to our fifth child by an emergency c-section, and the following week my husband

---

Types of Support

❖ Family and friends

❖ Support groups; join an existing one, or start your own

❖ Newsletters and magazines

❖ Pen pals

❖ Computer network

❖ Professional teacher assistance

lost his job! Several back issues of *Home Education Magazine* had just arrived. I read and re-read articles about home schooling under difficult situations. It helped me see that others survived and even flourished during tough times.

Pen pals

My pen pals, whether home schoolers or not, support my home schooling. I see no reason for corresponding with someone who continually questions my motives and sanity for having my children learn at home.

Jocelyn Butler views pen palling as more than a support system. She considers it an inexpensive way to help her children learn geography and writing skills. Having pen pals has also encouraged her boys to collect stamps. The Butlers often trade interesting items with their pen pals, sending cotton, sharks teeth or ostrich feathers for something just as interesting in return!

Computer support on line

As a home schooling family, you and your children can always "go to the board" for support, the computer bulletin board, that is. America Online, Genie, CompuServe, and Prodigy are services you will at least want to check into if you have a modem, or plan on getting one.

Homeschool Connection is the primary home schooling forum on America Online. "Folders" of information are available to the home school parent. There are also live "chats," including at least one specifically for children. You communicate by typing and sending off one line at a time, and you see lines others have sent. Essentially the chats are like phone calls enabling communication with home schoolers from distant places. E-mail allows you to send large amounts of text which waits in the destination "mailbox" to be retrieved. Whatever on line service you select, you'll find some sort of conference area for home schooling. You will want to monitor your children's conversations. Unsavory characters often use their computers to entice youngsters. My brother discovered his ten–year–old daughter chatting with an adult male on a teen line. The man had been requesting her address. You may want to set your receiving software to allow only specified contact areas.

On line providers charge around ten dollars a month plus several dollars an hour for over five or so. If your connection number is long distance, you have that charge, too. For heavy users these services are not exactly low–cost. Some companies like Netcom offer only internet connection without the extra services. With them you may use e–mail, the web, and connection to certain databases. Expect to pay $20 per month for nearly unlimited connect time. I suggest ordering the trial memberships (usually free) to examine just what you get for your dollar. Those of us who are computer illiterate, or at least internet ignorant, appreciate interactive on line beginner's workshops, which walk us through the various steps for services like e–mail, message boards, chats and files.

6 Low cost activities

You may have heard the saying, "One can never be too rich or too thin." Although I don't quite agree on those two points, here is my own never–too–much statement: "You can never have too many books or ideas!" I am always looking for a great idea, and I love to share what has helped me. Many home schoolers keep notebooks for learning ideas. I keep a binder with clear sheet protectors to hold interesting articles. When I look for a special project for the children, or to remind myself about ideas for saving money, I appreciate my collection. Many of the following ideas were mentioned by several home schoolers. When applicable, I have credited specific ideas to the mothers who suggested them.

Half of the secret to successful home schooling on a budget is in the attitude of the families. The final section of this chapter, "General thoughts on learning," demonstrates how good perspectives influence methods of education. We can all learn by looking through the eyes of others.

> **Caution:** Dry beans are suggested in several idea items. We do not recommend using them around infants or toddlers because beans can get stuck in ears and breathing passages.

_____ *Mathematics* _____

Craft sticks as math manipulatives

Buy inexpensive craft sticks at a discount store and use them as math manipulatives. Have your child group them by fives, tens, and so on. Or glue five or ten beans onto each stick and use them that way. Your child can easily see that ten groups of ten equals one hundred.

Milk jug lids as manipulatives

Use lids of various colors for counting, stacking, grouping, or as markers for homemade games. Poker chips may be used in the same way.

Sorting games using egg cartons

Use empty egg cartons for sorting by labeling the bottom of each egg cup with a number. Have your child sort that number of beans or other objects into the cup. This helps with number identification. –*V.C., IA.*

Dot–to–dot pictures

Place a sheet of tracing paper over a coloring book picture. Make dots outlining the picture. Number the dots in sequence. Or let your child make a dot–to–dot puzzle this way for you.

Use nursery rhymes to teach number concepts

Use manipulatives to demonstrate nursery rhymes such as *One, Two Buckle My Shoe* or *Ten Little Indians.*

Make lima bean people

To introduce counting and math concepts, purchase a bag of large white lima beans and draw faces on them with a small–point permanent black marker. Make up stories about the lima bean people that introduce subtraction, addition, etc. (For example, 10 lima bean people were in the library and heard the phone ringing. 3 thought it was a

smoke alarm so left. How many lima bean people stayed?)
–K.J., IA.

Play grocery store

Put prices on empty food boxes and jars. Use play money or make your own and let your children "go shopping." Small coin-tokens are more fun.

Buy a cash box

A real cash box adds to the fun of playing store and is a great way to sort coins. Use play money or have your child count back real change at your annual garage sale.
–K.J., IA.

Make an abacus

String beads on stiff wires (perhaps from clothes hangers). Then drill holes in an old picture frame to mount the wires, and you have an abacus! –S.A., MS.

Try making your own beads by coloring Cheerios® with felt-tip markers or food coloring. Spray them with hair spray to make them stiff. Don't try this with infants or toddlers around. They just may eat your project!

Make your own math games

Teacher's stores charge as much as $15 for math dominos that could easily be made with index cards. (or the Styrofoam board mentioned later in this section) Adding machine tape can be used for number lines, and paper plates for clock faces. –J.W., IL.

Use graph paper for number alignment

Quarter-inch graph paper helps children line up their numbers. This is especially helpful when using decimals. –T.S., MI.

Buy games for teaching tools

Purchase games such as Hi-Ho Cherry-O® and Barrel of Monkeys® at a discount store or yard sale. They are very inexpensive, and good for teaching number concepts to younger children. *–V.C., IA.*

Play card games

Play card games such as War or Crazy Eights that reinforce mathematical concepts. Using math this way makes learning fun.

Measure things around the house

Give your child a tape measure or ruler and index cards with names (and/or drawings) of common household objects. Have your child write down the measurements on the cards.

Use your kitchen to apply mathematical concepts to real life

Double cookie recipes, and share the extra cookies with a neighbor. Cut two pizzas each in a different way, and let your child figure out which way makes bigger slices one–fourth, or one–eighth.

Use waiting time to count with your children

Count to 100 when waiting in the car with the children. Ask how far do you think you can count before the light turns green. Or count in the doctor's office waiting room. See how far you can count before your name is called.

Learning fractions from measuring cups

In the bathtub, let your younger children play with measuring cups and spoons, experimenting with measurements of water. Ask questions, like how many of the one–fourth cup amounts does it take to fill the one–cup measure.

Fractions taught from pie–shaped cut–outs

Buy one–color place mats and use a compass to draw circles on them. Cut the disks into halves, thirds, fourths, etc., and use them to show your child fractions. Have them figure out which piece of a pie would be larger; one-fourth or one-half, etc. Instead of place mats, you can buy poster board made with a Styrofoam core sandwiched between two sheets of paper. For a homemade compass, you can tie a string between a tack or nail (at the center of the circle) and your pencil, or use a strip of cardboard with a hole poked in it for the pencil and another for the nail.

Language/Reading

Don't automatically purchase an expensive reading kit
Before you purchase $200 or more for materials that promise to help your child learn to read, check out other options. Many good books retail for less than $15.

Use an egg carton for sorting letters
Label sections with small letters. Have your child match the small letter with plastic magnetic capital letters. –*V.C.*, *IA.*

Make your own flash cards
Use blank index cards and a black marker to make alphabet, vowel, or word cards. Laminate them with clear adhesive shelf paper if you want them to last longer.

Label household items
Tape labels to items such as a chair, couch, table, Leave the labels up a few days and then remove them. See how many of the words your child can correctly identify.

Make your own books
Create a book using a blank scrap book or pre-punched large size index cards. Write a story with your child and either have him or her draw the illustrations or use magazine pictures. Write a story about your family using old

photos that aren't quite good enough for the family photo album.

Make an alphabet scrapbook

Have your pre-reader write each letter at the top of a page and help him or her find pictures in old magazines or workbooks of items that begin with that letter. Paste the pictures on the correct pages. Your child will take great pride in the project. The book can be used over and over for lessons.

Purchase a used typewriter

Younger children will use it constantly and learn letters, keyboard skills, and writing skills without much effort. Don't spend money on a children's typewriter. I haven't found one yet that satisfies my children.

Make a word box

Have your beginner reader write down words on 3X5 cards as he learns them. Use a recipe-card file to hold them. Invent silly sentences with the cards or use them as flash cards. Use a different colored marker if you want to separate nouns, verbs, adverbs, etc. By the time your child outgrows the box, he'll have a pretty good grasp of reading.

Make a flip-book

Buy 3X5 cards that come bound together as a small notebook. Cut the cards into thirds. Making three stacks write vowels on the middle third, and consonants on the outside sections. Flip the sections to make different words. This helps with word recognition and phonics.

Use blank books

You can purchase books with all blank pages or you can make them. Use them for alphabet books, for a homemade reader using words your child has already mastered, or as journals. –*N.E., CO.*

Use Mad Libs® to reinforce the parts of speech

Use inexpensive Mad Libs books to reinforce parts of speech in a fun way, or make up your own stories leaving blanks for nouns, verbs, adverbs, and adjectives important to the story. See how funny the story is after you've filled in the blanks.

Make spelling lists from your child's own writing

I derive weekly spelling lists from my children's journals. Rather than a spelling book, the children keep their own list of words they know they haven't mastered and practice the words on their individual lists. When their list gets long enough I give a written test . –*C.D., MO.*

Write letters to family members

Make mailboxes for each member of the family. Leave little notes inside for each other. This encourages good will as well as practice with handwriting and letter–writing skills.

Play scavenger hunt

Write simple clues on index cards. The incentive to read them is the prize at the end of the hunt, which could be a new book!

Develop story ideas

For creative writing, try a five–minute brainstorming session with the children. Develop elements for a story and write them down. Then have your children write using those ideas. For only one child, you could write while your child is writing. Compare stories when you've finished, and see how different they are.

Use the newspaper

Check letter recognition by having your child color in all the vowels or circle the letter of the day. –*S.A., MS.*

Invest in one good grammar book

A Warringer's high school edition is wonderful as a

reference. You don't need a separate language book every year. One good spelling book is sufficient as well. *J.B., NC.*

Find more words from the letters of a chosen word

One game we call *How Many Can You Make*. My son or I pick a word from the dictionary, the longer the better, and we have 48 hours to find as many words as possible, using the letters from that word. No two–letter words are allowed, and no slang terms. *–D.S., CA.*

Play games that reinforce language skills

Scrabble® is a great game for developing vocabulary and spelling skills. For a twist, make a list of commonly misspelled words and award extra points for using those words in the game correctly spelled, of course. *–T.S., MI.*

Boggle® is another fun game for finding as many words as possible in a short time from letter combinations.

_____ *Science* _____

Take nature walks

Take along a tote bag for treasures you are apt to find: a feather, a pine cone, a huge green leaf. When you get home, examine and talk about them. School age children can read about a selected object and write a brief report.

Make a butterfly net

Use an old broom handle and scrap net lace. Tape the net to a wire coat hanger with thick tape covering the edges. *–S.A., MS.*

Organize a nature scavenger hunt

We regularly go on a "hunt and find" walk. I make up 3X5 cards with specific items listed to hunt for, such as pine cones or bird feathers. Or I will make the card more general, listing a particular texture to look for in nature. We take along a picnic lunch and sketch book and make a day of it. –*D.S., CA.*

Make a paleontology kit

Purchase a plastic shoe box and fill it with items useful for fossil digging: hammer, multi–purpose dental pick, goggles, clamps, heavy needles, paint brushes, ruler, magnifying glass, etc. –*C.D., MO.*

Save old jars for insect collections

Keep jars on a particular shelf for collecting insects, worms, etc. for projects. Your children will be more apt to hunt for insects when they have a ready container. Use nylon pantyhose for covering jars with insects inside. Use a strong rubber band to hold it in place. –*T.S., MI.*

Put the bugs in a sealable bag or in a sealed jar inside the freezer for 24 hours to kill them.

Dissect your dinner

For a thrifty science lesson on dissection, try dissecting a butchered chicken to study the bone structure, then cook and eat that day's lesson! –*G.M., MO.*

Ask your doctor for free charts

Your family doctor may have extra charts, diagrams and models from pharmaceutical companies that he would be willing to part with. –*N.Y., PA.*

Let your children experiment in the kitchen

Set out ingredients such as baking soda, vinegar and food coloring for the young experimenters. Expect a mess and lots of fun. Or let them decide what should be in a muffin recipe and actually bake their concoctions. Explain why they needed eggs or milk or whatever they failed to put in. My son has made some pretty tasty cookies this way!

_____ *Social Studies* _____

Ask for postcards from all over the country

Put an ad in a magazine or newspaper asking for postcards.

Make a region book

Make state or province folders, labeling one for each state and filling the folders with postcards and maps you have collected. Do some armchair traveling with the children, pulling out a file to peruse together. Or instead, materials could be collected from a trip. A story could be written with added information about geography and history.

Write to tourist bureaus

Send for tourist information from each area you are interested in. Write to the state's department of tourism for free information. Ads in travel magazines could help.

Purchase a map puzzle of your country

Try and get a puzzle that also shows extra information such as crops and state flowers.

Make a map place mat

Laminate maps with clear contact paper for an interesting place mat for your children.

Use local maps

Get a free or low-cost map of your community from the local Chamber of Commerce and mark your home and places of interest on the map. Take walks and visit historical sights, parks, etc., noting your travel routes on the map. –J.B., NC.

Find old maps

Pick up old *National Geographic* magazines at garage sales, library sales, etc., if only for the maps. My children love looking at the maps and it is fun to compare old maps with the new ones.

Make a timeline

Use freezer paper from the grocery store or fan-folded computer paper. I made space for three parallel lines of historical development: biblical/church, world, and American history. I then drew vertical lines to label every 100 years and marked the years. When we study a period or person in history, we note this on the timeline. We then draw a simple picture to represent key events or discoveries. The time line is on a wall at child height. Use white labels to write the dates and events on and stick them up in the appropriate space. –*N.E., CO.*

For reference, look in your library for *The Timetables of History*.

Supplement history textbooks with "real" books

Make history come alive by reading biographies of famous people and historical-based fiction aloud together. The books in the *Landmark Series*, the *We Were There* series, and the *Childhood of Famous Americans* series are excellent, and out of print. Search for them at used book stores and library book sales. For 25¢ or so, you have great supplemental reading.

Study genealogy

Genealogy is history. Develop an interest in your family tree, asking relatives for information. Make a family record book, keeping family letters and photographs in a binder. –*J.B., NC.*

_____ *Art* _____

Make a craft box

Fill it with glue, construction paper, yarn, markers, sponges, glitter, crayons and scissors. Fill another box with old magazines, catalogs, cardboard tubes, etc. Save rocks, shells, leaves, and even corn husks for crafts. –R.B., MN.

Make an art notebook

Order inexpensive art prints from a supplier such as University Prints, and start an art appreciation notebook. Glue a print on each page and describe the painting and write what you have learned about the artist. –S.W., MD.

Make colored rice for art projects

Color rice with a few drops of rubbing alcohol and food coloring. Put into a Ziploc® bag and shake. Colored rice works well for measuring, pouring or gluing on construction paper as an art project. –V.C., IA.

Get end rolls of newsprint

Ask your local newspaper office for end rolls to use for art projects, posters, and even as wrapping paper, after decorating with sponges and paints or rubber stamps and ink.

_____ *Management* _____

Make your own organizer

Use a three–ring binder, designing categories that will work for you. Don't be bound by someone else's $35 dollar organizational ideas. –J.W., IL.

Make chore cards

I have written on note cards the steps involved in each

chore assigned to my children. I covered these in clear contact paper to extend their wear. We have an allowance system based on these chores. –*R.B., MN.*

Play chore bingo

Create different bingo cards for your children to complete. Each space is a chore such as washing windows, vacuuming the car, writing a letter to an elderly friend, etc. Prizes for filling in a row can be a sleep–over with friends, a date with their dad. For a completely filled card you could give them cash. –*M.S., PA.*

_____ *Other home education ideas* _____

Collect free things

Encourage collecting items such as bookmarks, business cards, stamps, rocks, flowers, leaves, bottle caps, etc. Collections can be a wonderful avenue for learning more about wildlife, other countries, the earth, business, etc. –*J.B., NC.*

Encourage helpful hobbies

Encourage hobbies that need to be done anyway, and that teach a skill, such as sewing, gardening, cooking, carpentry, or writing. My boys enjoy cooking as a hobby and are getting quite good at it! –*J.B., NC.*

Pick up promotional items at business fairs

Attend business fairs, parenting fairs, and other activities where free promotional items such as rulers, pencils, etc. are given out. –*J.B., NC.*

At business fairs children can learn a lot by seeing the machines and services used by businesses. Often an admission fee is charged for people who do not represent businesses since the companies who rent the booths want to focus their investment efficiently. You might get free passes by promising to not scoop up the freebies unless they are offered. Also ask when fewer people are expected, and go then. Vendors without prospects in sight may take time to explain their products or services and you won't be seen as an obstacle to their basic objective.

Carry postcards with you

When you run into a free offer listed in a magazine or reference book or hear about an organization that might offer free educational material, you can jot down the address and send for it right away. –*M.S., PA.*

Buy supplies in bulk

Buy huge amounts of spiral notebooks and portfolios when they are on sale. Buy paper by the ream at a school supply store and split the cost with a friend. Compare prices in an office supply store. –*J.B., NC.*

Use your walls for posting educational charts

I use our kitchen wall as an on–going learning site. I put posters, Bible verses, pictures, etc. on the wall next to the table and my husband and I discuss what is up there during our mealtimes. We have had number charts to 100, a picture of an insect metamorphosis, days of the week, money, etc. I have made my own small posters with adding machine tapes. –*J.G., CA.*

Subscribe to several educational magazines

A few well–chosen magazine subscriptions can be a way for relatives to help out, even if those relatives may not be completely in favor of your educational choice. Solid magazines like *Cobblestone* for history, *Cricket* for literature, *National Geographic World,* and *Ranger Rick* for science will delight everyone. –*S.A., MS.*

Look at teacher's magazines

Study them at a school supply house or library and adapt ideas to fit your home school. Subscribe to one if you think it would save you money. –*E.F., MO.*

Extend the life of your books

When they are showing signs of wear and tear, use tape or glue ordered from library supply catalogs. Prevent wear by covering paperbacks with clear adhesive shelf paper. Call (800) 962–4463 and ask for the book repair catalog, from Demco, Box 7767, Fresno, California, 93747–7767.

Make card games for different subjects

Try a different kind of Go Fish game. Make your own on index cards, using pictures of whatever you might be studying at that time; state capitals, mammals, animals, flowers, plants, insects, etc. Make two of each picture on a copy machine. Use the same cards for memory or as flash cards. –*J.G., CA.*

Share your magazines

I photocopy articles I want from magazines so I can pass the magazine on to someone who might not be able to afford it. This way I can show good stewardship to my children and share my enjoyment of good magazines. *T.S., MI.*

Use window shades for homemade charts

I have used old window shades (the roll–up type) for charts. Permanent markers write well on these and the charts can be stored easily for later use. –*T.S., MI.*

Make a date with your child

Every so often we have special dates with our kids, one on one, which we do inexpensively by focusing on their interests, which helps them learn. It may be a sewing project with me, going to a fossil–digging site with their dad, bowling, bicycling, browsing in an antique shop, a walk in the woods, getting a video free from the library, etc. –*C.D.*, *MO*.

Make a home school yearbook

We made a yearbook similar to those in private and public schools. My daughter was the first-year editor and she wrote by-lines, edited her younger sister and brothers' papers, and chose what to put in. We took many pictures and put those in the yearbook as well. My daughter even did title pages by hand, using calligraphy and drawings. Our final copy was run off at the printer's for each student. We punched three holes in the sheets and used yarn to hold the pages together. This is a great way for children to show off their work to friends and family who want to know what they are doing. Each year I pick a different editor. –*T.S.*, *MI*.

_____ *General Thoughts on Learning* _____

To estimate how much we spend per year for education is difficult. We teach all year, and never have a set amount that goes into home education, per se. We are a single-income family so we make do with book sales, school supply sales, etc. We also share a lot of resources with other families. –*D.S.*, *CA*.

Our home schooling activities do not lend themselves to an easy answer as to how much we spend on school supplies per year, per child. Ours is a natural learning approach. Of course, we use pencils, pens, paper, and the like, but spend perhaps only $10 per year on those things. The equipment we use is also our living equipment such as sleeping bags, binoculars, spotting scope, fishing rods, etc. The cost varies greatly from year to year as our interests change, but we buy used or get free or fixer-uppers wherever possible. Our textbooks are old encyclopedias and some math texts which we are able to get on loan from the local school. Perhaps our only consistent expense is magazine subscriptions at an average cost of $60 per child per year. –*L.P., ME.*

My best recommendation is to try to center activities around what's on hand or what is easily available. . . . Curriculum goals may be met in a variety of ways and even modified somewhat to use inexpensive resources or ones already owned. –*L.B., CA.*

Home schooling saves us money! We use all yard sale clothes because the kids aren't under pressure to dress in the latest fashions. The same goes for haircuts. We don't have to worry about the cost of school lunches or convenience food suppers. We can vacation at off-season prices. Also, home schooling has given us a high standard of living, *not* defined by money. We have time together. Our children really get to know each other. We can eat real food, and grow some of it. We can watch our house be renovated, and do some of the work ourselves. We have time to spend on our own reading, music, Lego®-building, or whatever we want to do, when we want to do it. –*J.B., NC.*

We consider learning to be something that just happens when people are interested in what they're doing, what goes on around them every day, so we don't separate what we do into "learning" and "other," our whole family is learning all the time. –*H.H., WA.*

Once you've got it, take care of it. This is the most important part of saving in our school budget. I don't like to even think about how many games, flash-card sets, science projects, we've gone through because of lost or mangled parts. Now I have an established place for each school item. Our philosophy has changed from "get it as cheap as you can, and we'll make do" to "don't fall for every bargain you see." A few wise investments will add much more to your child's life. –*T.E., OR.*

We are just beginning our home school journey, and loving it. Every day brings something to learn. So many parents I talk to are afraid they can't home school because they aren't organized or disciplined, or structured, or whatever. I try to help them see that you don't need to be any of those things. You just have to open your eyes and mind to the possibilities. –N.J., ID.

Children are very creative and can do without all the whistles and bells being touted as necessary for learning. –N.Y. PA.

We believe that if it's at all possible to study a subject in its most natural or simple form, learning takes place most naturally and simply without the distraction of complex activities, re–enactments and crafty guises of the simple truth. If we want to learn about seeds and plants, we garden rather than read about it in a textbook. –M.L. OH.

Trust God to provide for you. If he wants you to home school, he'll make a way for you to do it. The glitzy, high-tech programs or materials may not come your way, but true education consists of more than the latest fad. –P.T., NC.

7

Organize to economize

Good organization is the ignition system for a successful home school. That is not to say all home schoolers are naturally well-organized. To organize a household where children are around all day is a great deal of work, but the effort is well worth it. Dozens of excellent books offer to help you get organized, and many of their ideas can be incorporated into your home schooling.

The Challenge

In this chapter, I will address common home school clutter hazards. Home schooling requires copious amounts of papers, books and supplies. Your confidence as a home schooling parent depends on how easily you and your children can locate these materials. A home learning center with live-in young scholars means many little in-progress projects here and there. It also means dishes piling up, endless mountains of laundry, and household messes developing in every corner. Add to that your supply of books, workbooks, games, flash cards, charts, maps, catalogs, newsletters, home schooling magazines, and files, and we are talking about a massive amount of "stuff"! If you have an entire room designated as a schoolroom, wonderful! Most of us don't have that luxury. Keeping a closet, some shelves, or just a corner of the house organized for schooling is a job, but keeping an entire room organized, as well as an entire house, is an awesome task!

Routing it out of the house

Clutter control doesn't have to be expensive. Sure, you could hire a "clutter expert," but you can do it yourself at a fraction of the cost. Summer vacations are great times to do a little de–cluttering, and make some extra money at the same time. We hold an annual yard sale every June, selling what seems like tons of toys, outgrown clothing, books, and household items.

Try the room–by–room method of de–cluttering. Start with the kitchen and work your way to the bedrooms and even the bathroom. Be ruthless. Pretend you are moving and don't want to move all that junk. Have boxes handy for sorting. Use one for selling at your sale, one for donating, and one for throwing away. Give yourself three or four weeks to prepare for the sale. You will want to wash the clothing, clean the toys, and label everything, Your children will be willing helpers, and eager sellers, if you allow them to keep the money their own things bring in. The money you make can buy educational items and organizational tools. If you can't stand the thought of holding your own sale, you can take items to a consignment shop in your area or donate them to a charity service such as a homeless shelter, the Goodwill, or the Salvation Army. When I look for things to discard, I follow the general rule that items not used for the past year, probably are no longer needed. Maternity clothes and a few generic baby clothes are the exceptions to this rule, as everyone knows what happens when you finally dispose of those!

For organizing, I like to use what I call the "Three–B's"; boxes, bins, and baskets. Much of what needs to be organized in our homes can be sorted into one of these, and the cost can be minimal. Sturdy cardboard boxes can be picked up free at a local print shop, drug store, recycling center, or grocery store. My favorite boxes are from printers. They are the perfect size for storing textbooks or files. I use boxes to store readers for future use, files of importance for our schooling including back–year files for each child, scrap paper, and workbooks and textbooks for future grades. Produce boxes are useful for out–of–season clothing and Christmas decorations.

Clutter

Clutter is one of the greatest enemies of efficiency and stealers of time — and that includes yours. . . .

Junk makes every job harder and makes cleaning take forever. Any project we tackle, from building to dismantling, will be slowed, dampened and diluted if we constantly have to fight our way to it in the midst of clutter. . . .

Junk (and junk projects and activities) prevents you from being free, available for action or opportunity. Too often the things we save and store — for sentiment's sake or because they might be valuable someday — end up being tombstones for us. . . .

Eliminate the junk around your house. It's one of the easiest ways to free yourself from household imprisonment.

I use the inexpensive fold–together boxes for each child's baby things including their baby books, greeting cards, baptism candles and engraved baby spoons. I figure one box each will hold everything we want them to take with them when they marry and have families of their own. These boxes store well under a bed. Smaller items can be sorted into brightly-colored greeting card envelopes. Check out card shops after each major holiday. The greeting card representatives who clean off the shelves often just discard the envelopes, and will likely give you plenty if you ask. I have a thoughtful sister-in-law who works at a discount store and tracks down the card representative for me now and then. I store stencils and stickers in them, and we use them for letters to pen pals, too.

I love plastic bins. The shoe box size, often on sale for under a dollar, is the most valuable to me for home school storage and organization. Each Spring, I "spring" for a couple more bins toward our home organization. I store flash cards and card games in one, rubber stamps in another, markers and colored pencils in yet another. We also use bins for stickers, gummed stars, red pencils, award certificates and other traditional teacher's stuff that is so fun to use. You would not believe the difference a nice storage container makes in how your shelves of school supplies or toys look! The larger size of plastic bin is great for storing art supplies or game pieces.

Do you have beat-up game boxes on your shelves? Mine looked awful and I was tempted to throw them all out, until someone told me about using labeled Ziploc® bags to hold pieces and directions for the various games; storing them in a large plastic bin, and then storing the game boards beneath the bin! What a great storage idea, and it takes up much less space than all those game boxes! Legos®, Tinkertoys®, and Barbies® can also be stored in plastic bins, as well as any toys with small parts. Storage bins can be labeled with large white stickers, if there contents are not already obvious. I also designate one plastic bin for each child for small personal items they might want to keep from prying siblings. You may save money by buying less well-known brand containers, or you might even use contact paper covered shoe boxes for some of your storage needs. Your children can decorate shoe boxes to store their own things and attach labels or pictures to identify the contents.

Pretty baskets can perk up a room while serving as

storage containers. I've picked up at garage sales baskets ranging in size from a small duck basket that holds our rings at the sink, to a huge wastebasket–size wicker that stores my daughter's out–of–season clothes in her bedroom. A large basket with a handle holds our magazines. At Christmas time I decorate it with red and green bows. Baskets in the bathroom keep washcloths and hand towels handy, a hanging baskets holds the hair dryer and curling iron, and baskets next to the phone book and note pads. A basket in our school area holds little books for the baby. We like functional and decorative baskets. My chicken basket in the kitchen holds tea bags, and a duck basket in my daughter's room is for hair ribbons.

Also consider the versatility of colorful baskets for organizing laundry. Large baskets can hold stuffed animals while the smaller ones are better for books or blocks. Many families designate a laundry basket for each child to encourage responsibility for their own clothing.

Proper Paper Places

Paper seems to make the biggest clutter in the houses of home schoolers. Getting paper under control is a big step toward organization. A woman I knew was saving *all* of her two sons' things, from their baby teeth to all their drawings and school papers. By the time her older son reached second grade, she had five huge boxes of his things stored in their small bedroom, and another three for her younger son! She couldn't bear to part with anything. This is storing clutter instead of dealing with it. Do keep samples of your children's drawings as they grow and develop and other things they will be happy to have when they marry and have children of their own. Keep summary school records and a few, special papers, copies of tests if you give them, Keep more school paper and records if you need them to show school authorities. For detailed records of your children's lesson plans, you might want to find a lesson planning form you like and use it every year. Books like Theodore Wade's The *Home School Manual* or Gayle Graham's *How to Homeschool* contain reproducible charts for lesson and chore planning. Kathy VonDyke's *The Home Education Copybook* is an entire book full of forms. Photocopy charts you find the most comfortable and punch them for a three-ring binder. Forms not published for the purpose of being copied are illegal to copy.

For a few dollars at a discount or office supply store, you can get a package of top-loading, clear sheet protectors for special papers like awards and certificates. Three-ring binders work well for storing *Weekly Readers* or articles of interest. You can start early, teaching your children to arrange things alphabetically by having files for various topics. When we ran a magazine ad asking for postcards and maps for our geography studies. We made 50 files, one for each state. We heard from over 700 people and our files were bulging so we shared some maps with other home schoolers. My oldest daughter labeled each file folder by state, organized them alphabetically, and helped me sort through the hundreds of postcards and maps to file each state's information. Now, if we want information on a state or country we turn to the file boxes.

File boxes or cabinets are wonderful tools for organizing our projects, correspondence (to keep track of our pen pals), barter records, expenses, and whatever you can imagine

Teamwork

An efficient home requires an organizational plan for chores. Chore charts abound on the market and might work for your family. Some families assign certain chores and everyone knows what is expected each week. Accountability is important, especially for the child who will try to get away with not completing assigned tasks. If you decide to use money as a reward, be prepared for the child who won't want to do anything that doesn't net a profit.

We have tried many methods of getting our children to help around the house and found two basic rules helpful; #1, If you make a mess, clean it up before you make another one, and #2, a general clean up is required in the evening before any television. I have seen my twelve-year-old daughter clean the entire living-room on her own just to see her favorite show. I have used an up-beat music cassette to cheer up a five-minute pick-up for the whole family. To this day, my fifteen-year-old grimaces when he hears the Oak Ridge Boys sing Elvira because we used that song to clean to for years! You'd be surprised how much better a room can look after only five minutes of six people picking up! (the baby doesn't pitch in much yet) If you are at a loss as to where to begin with getting your own children to help, read the book *401 Ways to Get Your Kids to Work at Home* by Bonnie McCullough and Susan Monson. With 401 tips and ideas, you'll be sure to find something that helps your family!

Plan Major Attacks

Count on using any breaks in your school year to catch-up with deep cleaning and organization. We have even dubbed Mondays as our catch-up day. We finish up assignments from the previous week, clean up the inevitable weekend messes and organize for the rest of the week. We also use Christmas break to reorganize our schoolroom, finish correcting or filing loose papers, and get a good start on the new year. This is also the time we evaluate our plans and discontinue anything that isn't working. Then in the Spring, we take at least a week to go through our materials, preparing to sell unneeded items at a curriculum fair or through a used curriculum supplier. It's a time to open up the windows, let in the fresh spring air and do some deep cleaning! Read Don Aslett's *Is There Life After Housework?* and his other books on housecleaning. The children can pitch in by rearranging their rooms and dusting their bedroom furniture.

Once you are feeling more organized, you'll be surprised at how much more smoothly your household runs, especially your schooling. If your house is very cluttered, don't expect it to be clean overnight. It took awhile to get that way, it will take almost as long to get it under control. But it can be done. Vow today to do it.

8 Your home-based business

> *A key reason for including a cottage industry in your children's education is to help them discover the practical need and application of the three R's in everyday living and to provide motivation for learning a bread-and-butter skill or way to earn a living even though they may later acquire another skill or profession. There is no richer way to develop self-worth than in uniting hand with head and heart in building manual skills.*
>
> From Raymond and Dorothy Moore in *Minding Your Own Business*, page 147. Used by permission.

Now that your children are at home, how about bringing your job home too? If you've considered it, you're not alone. The number of home businesses has grown by leaps and bounds in the past few years.

A home business combines naturally with home schooling. Families with a single income appreciate the extra cash, and their working together can benefit learning together. In their *Moore Report International* Raymond and Dorothy Moore regularly publish stories about home businesses. They strongly encourage work for children, even volunteer work. *Growing Without Schooling* also abounds with stories of children and youth as workers in their parent's business, and as apprentices.

The Story Behind Our Family's Business

Before my husband and I opened our used bookstore, I was in the habit of saving money. Being thrifty takes time and planning. As explained in an earlier chapter, I took my children to garage sales, had them clip coupons, and discussed purchases with them. I also worked as a free-lance writer, selling articles on parenting, refunding, and other subjects that interested me. Even a one-person enterprise like writing can be shared. My children often use our typewriter for their own projects while I am at the computer. My self-employment allowed me to stay home and teach them.

My husband and I had often talked of someday establishing a family business but realization of that day seemed as unattainable and as far into the future as did a hoped-for visit to Alaska or our children's raising sheep and chickens. Then my husband lost his job a week after our fifth child was born and things changed. Suddenly, my very small, part-time businesses became our sole income, one that couldn't begin to support a family of seven. While my husband searched for work, I researched home and small business opportunities.

I wish I could say that we quickly found our niche in the business world, but we suffered through more than a year of David's unemployment. Then we started working with a business consultant to plan for a used bookstore. While David had been frantically searching for a social work job, God's plans for our family were of a different sort. It is He who paved the way for a business we could truly love, and one that could be shared with our children.

David and I love good books, and we saw the need for a source of quality used books for other families. Most people lack the time or desire to search used book stores, thrift stores, garage sales, library sales, and auctions. We would offer them that service!

To begin our business we acquired a small loan from a generous relative. The business consultant was very leery of our start-up budget. He didn't know he was dealing with a couple of expert penny pinchers, and was surprised on opening day to see our pleasant, well-stocked store.

During those months of unemployment and planning, the children learned important lessons about life. They collected cans for money and dug deeper at the recycling center for extra coupons. They even donated their prized doll house to our store. By continued involvement, they are seeing their cooperation contribute to business success.

In a home business, parents can earn an income while remaining with their children. Even if the business is away from the family residence, the family can work together. Although my husband is manager, our entire family is involved. Our six-year-old may clean the toys in the children's area while our thirteen-year-old reads teen books we might want to sell.

Examples of Families Who Combine a Business With Home Schooling

Rick Boyer, in his book *Home Educating With Confidence*, stresses the importance of young people working in preparation for their future careers. He recommends training in a family business, apprenticeships, employment in areas of interest, or teen entrepreneurships. By involving his three oldest boys in his drywall business, he has seen, firsthand, the value of work for young people. His boys have learned adult skills, contributed to the family income, developed a sense of the value of money, and have acquired a skill that can support them if needed. Boyer comments that business is a "great school." The "report cards" are taken seriously.

Working as a family toward a common goal is an important benefit of a home business, according to Bob Schneider. Bob and his wife Linda run the Rainbow Resource Center, providing home schooling families with both new and used curriculum materials. (See Chapter 10.) The Schneider's six children are actively involved in the business, entering books into the computer system, sorting and shelving books, and helping fill customer orders. Bob's long-term goal of working at home full time has been realized, thanks to diversification and the promotion of their new products catalog.

Susan Dahlem operates a home bakery business. Her children help bake and sell cookies, cakes, pies, breads, candies and party foods to order. She and her daughter Jessica publish The *Country Homemaker*. The newsletter provides country recipes, household hints, and wise advice from Susan's kitchen. Subscribers will have a one-of-a-kind cookbook when they put the newsletter pages into their own binder, as I have done.

The children of Marsha and Dwight Ransom have learned construction skills by helping in Marsha's business, Ransom Enterprises. The Ransoms purchase houses to "rehabilitate" and sell for a profit. Marsha comments that her children have developed in self-esteem and have learned cooperation in getting jobs done. Plus they are earning their own money.

Each of these home schooling families has found a way to combine education with a business. Could it work for your family as well?

Getting Started in a Home Business

If you want to begin a small business but have no idea where to start, read a book like Barbara Brabec's *Homemade Money*. She has ideas and advice for home businesses, and her book can answer just about any questions you might have. Also Paul and Sarah Edwards have written several good books on self-employment. They often recommend hiring a babysitter but I feel this defeats the main purpose of a family business. Instead, choose a home business your children can participate in, or at least one conducive to frequent interruptions. We who are home schooling mothers have already discovered ways to keep our kids learning. We nurse infants while we teach phonics principles, sew buttons on while we check math problems, and entertain a toddler with an abacus while we teach science concepts to our older children. We have learned to teach fractions with measuring cups while baking and cooking and to use coupons at the grocery store for practicing addition and subtraction skills. It shouldn't be too difficult to adapt to running a business from our homes! When Dad can be involved in the home business, it takes some of the stress off an already busy mother. Children can learn to help run the business, too.

A Good Cottage Industry

❖ Can be operated well at home

❖ Allows time flexibility

❖ Does not require expensive equipment

❖ Involves minimal financial risk

❖ Tends to restore, not divide, families

❖ May be enjoyed by all

Adapted from *Minding Your Own Business* by Raymond and Dorothy Moore.

——✳——

Prior to beginning a business, parents should consider several important topics:

✔ First of all think of how a business would affect the family. Will it take too much time? Can the children do some of the work? If they can learn by participation, the advantages might outweigh disadvantages.

✔ If the home business is more of a one–person enterprise, will the children get the attention they need, and will the mother or father have energy left to spend on home schooling? If given the opportunity, I could write at the computer for hours. But my home teaching and toddler's needs would suffer. When my husband takes the children to the park for two hours, I can type guilt free. Or an extra long nap time for our youngest makes it easy for me to write while my older children do their own writing or reading. I have learned to snatch available moments. I carry a small notebook in my purse so I can jot down my thoughts, instead of relying on memory. Some of my best ideas have come while nursing our baby to sleep. At such times I can write for an hour or two non–stop. I believe that God gives me the words. They just flow too easily to be coming by only my own efforts.

✔ Calculate start–up costs. Many families don't have much extra money to invest. If your hobby is crafts you may need very little cash to turn it into a business. If you decide to critique and type college students' term papers, word processing equipment and business cards may be all you need. Whatever you decide to do, don't go into an unpayable debt to do it. An away–from–home business may entail a higher investment, but with smart planning you could see good returns in just a few months.

✔ Before finalizing your decision make tentative plans for building a clientele, for ways to attractively present your service or product, and for advertising. And by all means, get advice from people who understand the factors in business success.

✔ Read books and magazines about small or home businesses. Marketing strategies vary considerably. Make your business a learning adventure, for yourself and for your children. Answers come through experience, but try to avoid costly mistakes. Chances are, someone else has faced your situation. Learning from their experience can save you money. Before beginning our small business, my husband and I read dozens of books, attended small business seminars, and worked with a business consultant. We purchased almost 1000 books for our inventory before we read a book specifically aimed at used bookstore owners. The author warned against buying older book club editions as they were practically worthless. Imagine how we felt having just paid a hundred dollars for 140 book club editions! They quickly ended up on a fifty-cents sale table. We made a mistake and will certainly make more, but we won't make that one again.

✔ Continue to improve your business. I write daily and subscribe to two writing magazines. I also read a minimum of one book on the subject per month. Daily writing is essential. I can be working on a book in progress, writing an article, journalling, or just writing a newsy letter to a friend. I try to write enough to keep at least one article waiting for an editor's consideration. If an article is rejected, I rewrite it immediately and send it elsewhere. I read voraciously. These are writing tips learned from experience, as well as from reading books and articles by successful writers.

Whatever your business, you can learn from someone who has gone the same route before you. Be an example to your children and show them that learning doesn't end when you receive a diploma!

If, after considering a home business and having cut corners in other ways, you are still short on cash, you may just need to find other ways to save money. The next chapter discusses ideas for trimming your family budget.

9

Other ways to save money

In what areas of your budget could you save more money? What are you willing to do without? Honestly assess your current standard of living, and ask yourself these questions. Juggling money to pay bills is an art in today's economy, especially for a one wage–earner family. I am eternally grateful to my parents for their thrifty examples and resourceful ways. Because my parents always put people before things, I am a better person. It doesn't take much to make me happy: a particularly good buy at a garage sale, bright white diapers on a clothesline blowing in the breeze of a sunny day, or the feel of hot black dirt burning the soles of my feet as I weed a garden. And by sharing pleasures with my children, they too can learn to appreciate the simple things in life. I feel sorry for children whose every material wish is satisfied while lacking quality parental attention. Think what they are missing!

Many home schoolers have financial constraints because a single income demands getting the most for your home school dollar. Some home schoolers are like Marion Cohen. She takes advantage of free community activities and low–cost books at thrift stores but she doesn't see it as home schooling on a shoestring. "If I were rich, I'd do it the same way." she explains. Home schoolers such as Cohen know the value of a dollar, and have learned what is really important in life. The simple things they scrounge up at thrift stores and garage sales add to their children's education and enjoyment without leaving a dent in the pocketbook.

Numerous books on the market demonstrate ways to save money. In the resources chapter I have listed several you may look for in your local library. They can help you work at saving money in general areas like food, clothing, and entertainment. Money saved in one part of your budget can feasibly be funneled to another, such as your children's educational interests. If you have always wanted to travel, if you'd love to be able to purchase a fancy microscope, or if you're finding too much month at the end of your money, this chapter is for you!

Affordable Food

How much do you spend on food? If you don't know, start saving all your receipts in an envelope in your purse. Make sure you write down any fast–food or restaurant meals on the outside of the envelope. If you pick up a can of pop or a candy bar for the children, write that down, too. After a month, tally up your totals. You may be in for quite a shock! I know that when I don't take the time to write out a list and plan my shopping trips, I can easily spend $15 to $25 more a week than I normally would. That's over $700 a year! I can't afford *not* to plan my shopping trip; can you?

Keeping an eye out for true bargains at your local grocery store or warehouse market can really pay off, especially if you buy in bulk when the price is right. Jane Wood adopted a money–saving idea from Amy Dacyczyn, editor of the *Tightwad Gazette* newsletter. She keeps a notebook where she lists typical prices at area grocery stores on the items she normally buys. This price guide helps her see if something is a really good price when it goes on sale. When commonly used items hit rock–bottom prices, she stockpiles.

Typical food costs

American families typically spend from $6,000 to $15,000 each year for food. The average per person is $1,600. $89 goes for cola drinks, $87 for cereals, $86 for ground beef, $85 for cheese, and $81 for milk. A typical family spends more than $1100 eating out.

Information from *Cut Your Spending in Half Without Settling for Less.* by the editors of Rodale Press, 1994.

Rhonda Barfield combines warehouse shopping, bulk buying, gardening, and other saving strategies to feed her family of six on $50.00 a week. Jill Bond does what she calls "mega–cooking" once or twice a year to fill her freezer with evening meals so she can spend more afternoon time with her family. As a bonus, she saves big money on the grocery bill. These actual home schooling mothers have found ways to save on one of the biggest money crunchers – food. They have written books so you can do it, too. Rhonda Barfield's *Eat Well for $50 a Week* includes many good recipes. Jill Bond's

Dinner's in the Freezer! is a household management tool full of helpful, money-saving ideas, great recipes, and working plans for mega-cooking.

Reaping Savings from a Garden

Growing a garden is one of the best ways to save money on your food bill. If you preserve your excess produce, the savings increase dramatically. Even if you don't can or freeze your garden goodies, your children can set up a roadside stand to sell extras and learn in the process. Better yet, allow your children free reign in a portion of the garden for their own creative crop.

If you don't have space for a full garden, plant seedlings in a box on the porch or in a small window box. What better living science experiment for the children? A box garden may not save on your food bill, but then you can visit a farmer's market and benefit from someone else's toil and sweat. Prices are usually less than in the grocery store, and nothing beats the fresh taste of locally-grown produce. I have never eaten a store-bought tomato that even came close to one right off the vine!

Coupons and Refunds

Couponing is another way to save money on your grocery bill. If you live in an area that doubles coupons, the savings potential is astronomical! Even without the option of double coupons, I regularly save 30% on my grocery bill. I obtain extra coupons from family and friends, and regularly sift through the newspapers in our community recycling center for extra inserts. Of course, check first to be sure this sort of scavenger hunt is legal in your town.

I was well-known at a previous recycling center and the workers told me they were surprised at how many people would dig through the bins for one reason or another. I am

Ways to Save Money on Food

- ❖ Warehouse shopping
- ❖ Bulk buying
- ❖ Large-scale planning
- ❖ Shopping from a menu
- ❖ Cooking large batches of meals
- ❖ Gardening
- ❖ Couponing and refunding
- ❖ Stockpiling
- ❖ Home food preparation

sure they were amused more than once by my family's excursions to their center as even the baby got involved by going for coupon inserts mom couldn't quite reach! My goal is to collect ten to twenty high-value coupons to use when the item goes on sale. This is how I am able to stockpile as many as twenty boxes of cereal for nineteen cents each, or twenty tubes of free toothpaste. With five children, I know I will use these items eventually or will be adding excess stockpiled items to Christmas baskets.

Couponing takes time and organization, but the children can help clip, alphabetize and file. Many home schoolers use coupons in their trips to the grocery store to involve their children in real-life math skills. Children can compare prices to figure out if the generic option would still be a better deal. Coupons do *not* save money if you use them simply because you have them, for items that are high-priced or that you wouldn't normally purchase. Disposable diapers with a $1 coupon off are still more expensive than cloth diapers, and frozen dinners for fifty cents less are still more expensive than cooking from scratch. If you normally purchase those items, by all means cash in on the savings with coupons. But if money is tight, you may want to rethink your spending habits.

Refunding carries couponing one step further, by taking advantage of rebates and premiums that many companies offer on their products. In some years 80% of my Christmas gifts were free through refunding. Refunding requires saving all the boxes and packaging of brand-name products you use, anticipating offers the companies are bound to have. Some offers require a specific time frame of purchase and a dated cash register receipt, but others request only a specific number of universal product code symbols (UPC's). This is how I was able to get twenty sets of Christmas lights a couple of years ago after inheriting a qualifier collection from an M&M® lover! Those light sets made great Christmas gifts and were later offered in stores for $9.00 a set! Refunders eagerly anticipate such offers! I have received T-shirts, soccer balls, basketballs, cameras, books, hats, sunglasses, watches, stuffed animals, maps, art sets and even a video camera free through my refunding.

The hobby can be time consuming and it requires organizational skills, but again, it can provide a learning experience for your children. Liz Perkins encourages her daughter, Melissa, to save UPC's for gifts she would like. Melissa recently saved for a collector Barbie doll for herself, as well as for a Christmas gift for her brother.

Anyone interested in learning more about refunding can order a refunding newsletter such as *Refund Express* or *Refunding Makes Cents*. These magazines list current offers, give tips on organization and saving money, and contain funny stories and articles from subscribers. Both have ads for trading with other refunders.

You can save on food costs by mega-cooking, buying in bulk, shopping at warehouses, gardening, or couponing. Let's next consider ways to save on clothing.

What people pay for clothing

✦ Men in the US spend an average of $345 a year on clothes. For women, the figure is nearly double – $607.

✦ $120 of what women spend is for shoes, $118 for dresses, and $117 for jewelry.

✦ $80 is spent for boys, $105 for girls.

✦ Each household spends $70 for dry cleaning.

Information from *Cut Your Spending in Half Without Settling for Less.* by the editors of Rodale Press, 1994.

Cutting Clothing Costs

A definite benefit to schooling your children at home is that they will probably not be demanding expensive designer duds as do children surrounded by peers. If your family wants to live in sweat pants, and you spend most of your day at home, who cares what you are wearing? If you spend your day gardening in bonnets and pinafores, that is fine too. You may remember, as I do, sneers and taunts of classmates who criticized clothing different from the latest style.

Garage and yard sales are favored sources of clothing for home schoolers and a great way to get quality clothing at a fraction of the original cost. I am often indebted to the double-income baby boomers who limit their families to only one or two children. I am able to purchase for only a dollar or two, outgrown clothing that cost them a mint at specialty children's stores. I often find high quality articles with very little wear which I can pass down several times.

**Ways to Cut
Clothing Costs**

✦ Plan your purchases
✦ Buy at yard sales
✦ Buy at consignment
   stores
✦ Buy at thrift stores
✦ Accept from friends
✦ Make your own
✦ Repair your own

Garage saling is a fine art, requiring early morning excursions for the best selections. Prepare a list of items that you really need for the next season. Impulse purchases can add up. Do you really need three pairs of size 10 boots, or will one pair do? What about the doorstop shaped liked Lincoln's head? Wouldn't it be wiser to spend the ten dollars on winter coats for two of your children? You may find when winter arrives you lack the forty dollars or more for a brand new one. A periodic inventory of your children's clothing needs helps your money management. Each season I clean out drawers, save what will be handed down, sort out what I will sell, and make a list of what to look for during the next garage sale season.

What I can't find at garage sales I can often pick up at used clothing consignment stores. Because these shops are usually very selective, you can expect good quality. Prices will be higher than at garage sales due to business overhead, but still you are not apt to pay more than half of the original prices. Consignment shops are a good place to find specialty items such as suits, dress shoes and snowsuits.

Another good clothing source is relatives or friends who are willing to save outgrown clothes for you. A good friend was a tremendous help to me in this way for three years.

Sewing saves money on clothing, even if your skills are limited to mending. And it is an educational experience for your children. If you are really creative, you can even make your own patterns or modify patterns to fit several young-sters. My own mother's creations fascinated me. She made jumpers from her own used clothes for my sisters and me, and used leftover cloth to create original Raggedy Ann dolls and teddy bears. I still have the gray teddy bear she made me out of my favorite coat!

Pleasure for Pennies

Entertainment comes easily for home schoolers. Responses to my questionnaire indicate that our children are very creative and adept at finding ways to enjoy life. They tend to like board games. Several mothers said they make their own versions of favorite games or invent their own. Renee Bjork receives school supply catalogs and brainstorms as she pages through them, jotting down ideas for making similar items for little cost.

Top Ten Toys
(choices of parents surveyed)

❖ Legos®
❖ craft boxes
❖ clay
❖ wooden blocks
❖ model kits
❖ science kits
❖ board games
❖ videos
❖ books
❖ siblings
(no batteries needed)

The top ten toys, rated for their educational and entertain-ment value, were; Legos,® craft boxes full of art supplies, clay, wooden blocks, models, science kits, board games such as Scrabble® and Monopoly,® videos, books (of course!), and siblings! None of these need be terribly expensive and most can be bartered for, found at garage sales, or bought at a discount, except the siblings!

Family outings can also be inexpensive. Why not save the cost of going out for a meal by packing a picnic lunch and taking the family to a park? Museums, zoos, and free concerts enrich your family's life without spending a lot of money. Beth Garcia finds that a yearly membership fee to a museum pays for itself through members–only reduced fees on classes and books. Educational television is, by far, the most often viewed by the home schoolers I corresponded with. Booklets and pamphlets offered free to teachers may also be available for your home classroom. The supplemental materials can enhance the learning from these educational programs.

Today, many parents on the fast track feel the need to shower their children with material things to make up for not spending time with them. They choose to have a bigger house or a fancy car rather than getting by with a single family income so one parent can stay home with the kids. As home teachers, we have already chosen to give our children the time. That likely means we must decide what else they really need and what they can do without. It means looking realistically at the difference between luxuries and necessities. Caring about our children provides incentive to discover how to save money.

> Poverty is, to some degree, an attitude. Notice the words of the Apostle Paul:
>
> *"I have learned, in whatsoever state I am, therewith to be content." (Philippians 4:11, KJV)*

10

Where to find what you need

This chapter lists resources I have tried or reviewed myself. If a costly resource is listed, it is only because I found it to be well worth the money. I have included a few items with prices that exceed budgets such as mine. They are to consider for your wish list or to borrow by interlibrary loan. In some cases, support group orders would make more-expensive items affordable with a group discount.

Resources appear here in seven general categories and are divided further within each one. The categories are: (1) teaching methods, (2) teaching support, (3) teaching and learning materials, (4) special learning experiences, (5) home and school organization, (6) home businesses, and (7) saving money.

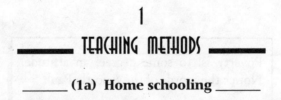

1
━━━ TEACHING METHODS ━━━

_____ (1a) Home schooling _____

When you first start home schooling you may be tempted to buy every home school book on the market. Resist the temptation. Instead, check your local library or use interlibrary loan to read the books you see recommended. If you find yourself renewing one particular book several times or resisting the urge to highlight everything, consider purchasing the book for your home library. I find myself referring to the books I own many times throughout the year, and the information within them has paid for the books several times over. This list is by no means comprehensive. The following books are those that were most often recommended by other home schoolers, and the ones I have found most helpful.

Christian Home Educators' Curriculum Manual by Cathy Duffy. (Two editions; one for elementary grades, and one for high-school), Home Run Enterprises, 1995. 16172 Huxley Cir., Westminster, CA 92683. Phone (714) 841-1220 Fax (714) 841-5584. E-mail: Caduffy@aol.com. An excellent manual in which Cathy reviews thousands of products. "It helps us learn how to select curriculum for each of our children and put together a comprehensive, goal-oriented program."

Good Stuff: Learning Tools for all Ages by Rebecca Rupp, Home Education Press, 1993. $14.75 plus $2.50 shipping and handling and 3.50 for first class. MC/Visa accepted. Order from Home Education Press, P.O. Box 1083, Tonasket, WA 98855. (800) 236-3278. E-mail: HomeEdMag@aol.com. This book is a wonderful resource reference book, listing thousands of books, magazines, catalogs, videos, games and other items for home schoolers or any other educator. You can use this book to *save* money by reading extensively about a product before you order it from a catalog or supplier.

Home Educating With Confidence by Rick and Marilyn Boyer, The Learning Parent, 1995. $9.95 plus $2.50 shipping and handling. Order from: The Learning Parent, Route 3, Box 543, Rutsburg, VA 24588. As parents of twelve home educated children, the Boyers believe that learning is a natural function that can happen better at home than anywhere else. I loved this book! I highly recommend it for parents of home educated children, whether they have been teaching at home for twelve days, or twelve years! In other words, there is encouragement and support for everyone in the Boyer's book.

The Home Education Copybook by Kathy Von Duyke, 1994, KONOS Helps!, 2285 Pleasant Valley Rd., Newark, DE 19702. A non-consumable, copy-ready planner full of forms of every conceivable kind. Use this year after year to make your own teacher's planners. Great for those of us who need to write things down to keep ourselves organized.

The Successful Homeschool Family Handbook by Raymond and Dorothy Moore. Moore Foundation, Box 1, Camas, WA 98607. (360) 835-5500. This book helped me through some rough times in our home schooling. A good book for encouragement and support of the home schooling lifestyle. Real-life examples of how others overcame burnout.

The Home School Manual by Theodore Wade, and others. 6th edition, Gazelle Publications, 1995, 1996. A must-read for home educators. This thick book covers every subject imaginable, with plans, pointers, advice and an extensive resource section. [And there is an easy-to-use, electronic edition for Windows, too, for only $18 postage paid. (Ed.)]

The Home School Source Book by Donn Reed, Second Edition, revised. Brook Farm Books, 1994. $15.00 plus $1 postage. Send to: Brook Farm Books, P.O. Box 246, Bridgewater, ME 04735. This book is an extensive review of home school supplies and books, as well as a wonderful collection of articles and essays by Donn Reed.

Homeschooling For Excellence by David and Micki Colfax, Warner Books, 1988. If you're new to home schooling, you may not have heard about the home schooled Colfax boys who went to Harvard, but for the rest of us, the Colfaxes have remained an icon of home school success.

How to Create Your Own Unit Study, and The Unit Study Idea Book, both by Valerie Bendt, Commonsense Press, 1994. Both of these books are available through the Bendt Family Ministries, 333 Rio Vista Ct., Tampa, FL 33604. Request their free catalog. Excellent books for those who are interested in using a unit-study for their home classrooms.

How to Homeschool by Gayle Graham and Linda Trumbo. Commonsense Press, 1992. 5903 Grove Ave., Richmond, VA 23226. E-mail: CYGR41B@prod.com. A very practical, easy-to-understand guide which includes reproducible charts for organization. You may also send for a free quarterly newsletter.

How to Stock a Home Library Inexpensively, 3rd edition, by Jane A. Williams, Bluestocking Press, 1995. $14.95 plus $2.50 shipping and handling. P.O. Box 1014, Dept. 3H, Placerville, CA 95667. (800) 959-8586. Fax # (914) 642-9222. Jane Williams discusses the importance of a home library and tells how to stock one at low cost. Excellent resource for all book lovers.

How to Write a Low Cost/No Cost Curriculum by Borg Hendrickson, Mountain Meadow Press, 1990. Mountain Meadow Press, P.O. Box 318, Sitka, AK 99835-0318. Encourages the parent to evaluate their own goals and objectives for their children's education and gives guidelines and ideas for designing an inexpensive, individual curriculum.

The Successful Homeschool Family Handbook: *A Creative and Stress-Free Approach to Homeschooling* by Raymond and Dorothy Moore, Thomas Nelson Publishers, 1994. Or from Box 1, Camas, WA 98607. (360) 835-5500. This book presents many real-life examples of different approaches to home schooling and shows what works and what doesn't. A must-read for home schoolers who are still searching for a method that will work for their family or for those who want reinforcement and support for the choices they have already made.

You Can Teach Your Child Successfully, *Grades* 4-8 by Ruth Beechick, Arrow Press, 1992. 8825 Blue Mountain Dr., Golden, CO 80403. $14 postpaid, paper. Down to earth advice on teaching your children the basics. My mother loaned me this book three years ago and I have yet to return it because I find myself referring back to it several times a year.

The WholeHearted Child. By Clay and Sally Clarkson, Whole Heart Ministries, P.O. Box 228, Walnut Springs, TX 76690. $20.95 plus $3.50 shipping and handling. Revised and expanded, 1996. This handbook shows how to use whole books and real life to teach and train children ages 4 – 14 at home. In it you will find hundreds of practical ideas. I loved it and expect to refer back to it many times!

____ (1b) Other helpful books for home teachers ____

As an avowed book lover, I couldn't complete this chapter without including the titles of some very influential books which, although not directly pertaining to home schooling, support a home learning lifestyle.

All The Way Home: *Power For Your Family To Be Its Best* by Mary Pride. Excellent book that is the sequel to Mary's equally thought–provoking book, *The Way Home.* Subjects dealt with include home education, time management and family work. Practical wisdom from other families is included.

The Book of Virtues edited by William J. Bennett, 1993, Simon & Schuster. Rockeffeller Center, 1230 Avenue of the Americans, New York, NY 10020. A treasury of moral stories divided by subject; friendship, responsibility, compassion, honesty, work, etc. These stories and poems are wonderful for reading aloud.

Dumbing Us Down: *The Hidden Curriculum of Compulsory School-ing* by John Taylor Gatto, New Society Publishers, 1992. If you are unsure about home schooling, or need some answers to concerned relatives who fear your children will become pariahs [low social caste] of society if they are home schooled, read this book. It reinforced my decision to home school. Like Gatto, I don't believe a classroom of 30 peers is the ideal learning environment. Ironically, Gatto is a public school teacher!

What Your 1st Grader Needs To Know: *Fundamentals of a Good First-Grade Education,* by E.D. Hirsh, Jr., Doubleday, 1991. This is first in a series of six books, one for each grade up to the sixth. They are great to fill in weak areas in your curriculum and for reading aloud. They give you a good idea of what your kids should know at each grade level. I've checked them out from the library many times. When the full line is available in the less expensive paperback editions, I plan to buy them.

Your Money or Your Life by Joe Dominguez and Vicki Robin, Viking Penguin, 1992. 375 Hudson St., New York, NY 10014. Think you are making a living with your job? Think again. If you are working at a job you hate, ignoring your life's dreams, or working just for the money, then this book shows you how you are actually "making a dying" with your job. You'll never look at money or career choices the same way again.

2
TEACHING SUPPORT

_____ **(2a) Magazines** _____

When I began home schooling, I subscribed to every newsletter and magazine on home schooling that I could find, thinking more is better. After a year I could see which magazines actually gave me ideas or the support I so desperately needed as a new home schooler. What I should have done is send for a sample issue of each one. Don't go broke subscribing to several different magazines. Check them out and see which one, if any, will fit your family's needs. This list is fairly comprehensive and includes magazines and newsletters I no longer subscribe to. They are listed so families can compare prices and send for samples of any that appeal to them.

Bright Spark Super Learning Tools, 20887 N. Springs Ter., Boca Raton, FL 33428–1453. (407) 487–3199. E–mail: BrghtSprk@aol.com. Monthly newsletter. $7.50 a year, 12 issues. Each issue has home schooling hints and tips, interviews, recipes, discount information, and product information. Editor Alison Moore Smith writes excellent articles. Well worth the subscription fee.

Christian Home Education News, P.O. Box 977, Pinellas Park, FL 34664–0977. $10.00 for 12 issues. Editor Roy Lind. Newspaper format. Articles, news updates, ads. Send for a free sample copy.

Family Learning EXchange; *Journal of Natural Learning, Family Learning, and Homeschooling*, P.O. Box 300, Benton City, WA 99320. Published by Janie Levine, bimonthly, 1 year $15.00, 2 years $25.00. (509) 588–2627. A smaller newsletter–type format with columns, product reviews and comments and ideas from readers.

Family Unschoolers Network (F.U.N.) News, 1688 Belhaven Woods Court, Pasadena, MD 21122-3727. Edited by Nancy and Bill Greer. $8.00 a year, 4 issues. This little newsletter is just what it says–"Fun." It is not intended to replace other publications, only to supplement them with articles you won't see elsewhere, resources, ads, and ideas. *The Family Unschooler's Network* "believes learning should be fun for the whole family." Articles from all ages are welcome.

Growing Without Schooling, 2269 Massachusetts Avenue, Cambridge, MA 02140. HoltGWS@aol.com; Compuserve: Go edline; Forum B. A bimonthly newsletter. $25.00 for one year, an additional $3.00 for Canada. Initially begun by John Holt to support families who chose natural learning or unschooling for their children. Editor Susannah Sheffer continues the newsletter in the spirit of the late John Holt. Full of stories and examples from home learning families. Back issues available for a fee and could serve as an educational tool for the teacher.

Heart of Homeschooling, P.O. Box 7275, Fairfax Station, VA 22039. E-mail : ShariHeny@aolcom. One year (6 issues) $17.16, or $29.95 for two years. Single copy $4.00. Order line: (800) 600-3633. An "infant" publication that premiered in May of 1995, I sent for a sample because I loved the articles I had read by editor Shari Henry. She hasn't disappointed me. *Heart of Homeschooling* is "devoted to affirming and emboldening home schooling families. We believe children's natural curiosity about the world around them should be gently guided in an environment of love, security and freedom, with respect given to each child's gifts, temperaments and developmental abilities." Enough said.

Home Education Magazine, P.O. Box 1083, Tonasket, WA 98855. E-mail: HomeEdMag@aol.com. (800) 236-3278. MC/visa accepted. One year subscription (six issues)–$24.00, single issue sent first-class $4.50 Canadian orders, add 35%. Editors Mark and Helen Hegener offer a diverse selection of articles in this bimonthly magazine. With regular columnists and reviews. I find this magazine to be informative, well-balanced, and helpful to the novice or seasoned home schooler.

Home School Digest, P.O. Box 125, Sawyer, MI 49125. Published by Wisdom Publications, this magazine has a definite religious slant. Informative articles and inspirational essays from regular columnists and home schooling parents. Write for information about a two-for-one subscription price they have offered in the past. $18 a year, 4 issues.

Home School Times, P.O. Box 2807, Napa, CA 94558-0280. (800) 600-3633. $17.16 for one year (six issues) or $29.95 for two years. Christian family magazine for the home school lifestyle. Published bimonthly by Jan and Greg Parrish. I love the reviews and resources listed in this smaller magazine. Some excessive use of clip-art and font-style bothers me a little but I can look beyond it to the helpful information within the magazine's pages.

Homeschooling Today, P.O. Box 1425, Melrose, FL 32666. Order line: (954) 962-1930. E-mail: HSTodayMag@aol.com. Bimonthly, $17.95 per year $25.95 per year, Canada. Christian focus with helpful articles. A unique feature is their "pull-out" art selection designed as a tool for teaching art study. Also a question/answer section with Dr. Ruth Beechick.

Moore Report International, The Moore Foundation, Box 1, Camas, WA 98607. (360) 835-5500. Newspaper format, edited by Dorothy Moore, a home schooling movement pioneer with her husband, Raymond. Timely updates on home schooling topics in the news, letters from subscribers, columns by the Moores and various other home schooling writers. $12 for one year (six issues), $20.00 per year, Canada or Mexico, one free sample issue on request.

Practical Homeschooling, Home Life, P.O. Box 1250, Fenton, MO 63026–1850. E-mail: phscustsvc@aol.com. (800) 346–6322 Fax (314) 343–7203 $19.95 for six issues (one year). Edited by Mary Pride. Good columns and regular features, including helpful reviews of educational products. The reviews of computer products got so big that Mary launched a new publication, *Homeschool PC*, in the fall of 1995. *Practical Homeschooling* is full of useful information.

The Teaching Home, P.O. Box 20219, Portland, OR 97220–0219. $15.00 a year, $20.00 for Canada, bimonthly. The purpose of *The Teaching Home* magazine is "to provide infor-mation, inspiration, and support to Christian home–school families and organizations". Publishers are Pat and Sue Welch and family. I enjoy the "Letters" section the most, with feedback and ideas from other home schoolers.

____ (2b) Home school support organizations ____

You can find state-by-state listings of home school support groups in many home school books such as Ted Wade's Home School Manual, or you can acquire a directory of many home school organizations from Growing Without Schooling . Mary Pride's Big Book of Home Learning also lists state organizations. The state organizations (listed by Wade, Pride, The Teaching Home, Growing Without School-ing, and Home Education Magazine) have the most complete and up-do-date information on local groups.

National Center for Home Education, P.O. Box 159, Paeonian Springs, VA 22129, (17333 Pickwick Dr., Purcellville, VA 22132); (703) 338–7600; Fax (703) 338–2733. Michael Farris, President/Director; Douglas Phillips, Director of Govern-ment Affairs. The Center was founded by the Home School Legal Defense Association to serve state leaders by dissemi-nating pertinent government and legislative information related to home schooling on a monthly basis. HSLDA fully funds the Center as a subsidiary ministry. NCHE's services are available to any state organization upon request and without charge. In addition to monitoring legislation on the state and federal levels, the Center works on special public relations projects involving home schoolers. These include clarifying the viability of this education choice to concerned officials, promoting proper understanding of methodology and standardized test scores, communicating with the media to avoid misunderstandings, and holding regional meetings for support group leaders.

National Homeschool Association, P.O. Box 157290, Cincinnati, OH 45215-7290. The purpose of the National Homeschool Association is to "advocate individual choice and freedom in education, to serve those families who choose to home school, and to inform the general public about home education." Membership is open to all interested persons. Benefits of membership include a subscription to the newsletter, *The NHA Forum*, networking and referral. Write for information on membership or for a referral to state wide organizations.

Home Education League of Parents, 3208 Cahuenga Blvd. W., Los Angeles, CA 90068. HELP serves all home school parents regardless of their philosophy and provides information on alternative education programs and groups. Emphasis on child-directed activities. (818) 508-8066.

____ (2c) General magazines and newsletters ____

I'm as addicted to magazines as I am to books — both wholesome diversions. But subscribing to all the magazines and newsletters that interest me would leave us broke. When viewing magazine subscriptions for my children as a school-related expense, I'm more apt to justify their purchase. We don't subscribe to the slick women's monthly magazines because they do little to reinforce the choice of full-time mothering, much *less home schooling. The following magazines are either educational in nature, or supportive of a home schooling lifestyle. The resources that are marked * were highly recommended by the home schoolers in my survey.*

An Encouraging Word, 1504 Cleveland Street, Idabel, OK 74745. A wonderful little magazine published by Nick and Cathrine White, a home schooling family of five. The articles are meant to encourage the Christian woman at home. $12.00 a year for four issues.

The WholeHearted Mother, P.O. Box 228, Route 1, Box 617A, Walnut Springs, TX 76690. $14.00 a year for 12 – page quarterly. This is the newsletter produced by publishers of the book, *The WholeHearted Child*. A journal for Christian mothers with children living and learning at home. Includes book reviews, home education and home discipleship tips and letters and ideas from subscribers. A beautiful and encouraging newsletter.

The Country Homemaker, 1685 San Antonio Ave., Many, LA 71449. Kitchen tips, recipes, and homemaker wisdom fill the pages of this lovely little newsletter by Susan Dahlem and her daughter Jessica. As you get the issues you can put them in a binder and eventually have an entire cookbook. Susan is a mother of six. $12.00 a year, for 4 issues, or a sample issue for $3.00.

Family Fun,* P.O. Box 10161, Des Moines, IA 50340– 0161. $14.95 a year (10 issues). The fun ideas for family activities and learning games make this magazine one of my favorite resources. While not designed with home schools in mind, a surprising number of the parents I surveyed recommended it.

Kids Discover,* P.O. Box 54206, Boulder, CO 80321–4206. Credit card orders accepted by phone: (800) 284–8276. Each issue covers a single subject such as Colonial America, weather and space. Our whole family loves it. $17.95 a year for 10 issues, for children ages 5–12.

Learning,* P.O. Box 51589, Boulder, CO 80321–1589. A teacher's magazine. $20.00 a year, 6 issues. The articles don't interest me nearly as much as the information on free offers for teachers and classrooms. The "Check It Out" column lists dozens of freebies or low–cost resources for teachers to participate in. Also of value are the pen pal listings and ideas shared by teachers.

National Geographic World, P.O. Box 2174 Washington, DC 20013. $14.95 a year, 12 issues. (800) 647–5463. Children's magazine for young geographers.

Pickwick Papers For Little Women, c/o Beth Kenyon, 445 South Brewer St., Manchester, IA 52057. You can get a sample for $1 or $5.00 for a year of six bimonthly issues. A newsletter written by and for home schooled pre–teens and teens with the focus on articles of interest to "little women." A good forum for home schooler's stories, poems, and articles.

Weekly Reader,* 3001 Citadel Drive, P.O. Box 8996, Delran, NJ 08370–8996. (800) 446–3355. An educational poster is occasionally mailed along with the magazine. While orders of ten or more copies are less expensive, two copies (one for student, one for teacher) are still affordable at less than $7.00 a year for the younger grades. Ask about subscribing and request a catalog of instructional materials such as Master Skills workbooks in math, reading and comprehension, or Map Skills booklets.

Zillions, *Consumer Reports for Kids,* P.O. Box 54861, Boulder, CO 80322. (800) 234–2078. A consumer magazine designed for children ages 8–14. One year (six issues) for $16.00.

3

TEACHING AND LEARNING MATERIALS

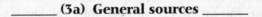

Many other sources of quality discount books are not listed here, and libraries offer free access to books. Of course some books you will want to shelve in your home library. From my own review and the recommendations of other home schoolers, catalogs of the suppliers which follow have the steepest discounts or the most helpful selections. Two asterisks (**) after company names identify the sources receiving the most recommendations from home schoolers I corresponded with for this book. Keep in mind that popularity depends partly on successful advertising.

(3a) General sources

Conservative Book Club, 33 Oakland Avenue, Harrison, NY 10528. This is my personal favorite in book clubs, and the only one I have ever continued ordering from after fulfilling my membership requirements! Very supportive of home schooling, the club often lists educational books at a discount. New membership offerings have included a set of Laura Ingalls Wilder books for shipping costs only or the Charlotte Mason set of books for a fraction of the usual cost. Look through your favorite home schooling or Christian magazine for their current offer.

Dover Publications,** 31 East 2nd Street, Mineola, NY 11501–3582. Beautiful and inexpensive books of all kinds: activity books, mazes, dot–to–dot books, books on mask–making, etc. A large portion of them retail for only $1.00! Send for their catalogs, especially the children's catalog.

The Elijah Company, Route 2, Box 100–B, Crosssville, TN 38555. Phone (615) 456–6284 Fax (615) 456–6384. E–mail: Elijahco@aol.com Owned and operated by the Davis family, home schoolers themselves. Their catalog is full of wonderful books and products for home learning, each one personally tested and recommended by the family. Their catalog is also full of tips, hints, and great ideas. Free catalog.

Golden Book Club, P.O. Box 475, Ramsey, NJ 07446–9912. Request catalogs for the grades you teach. Inexpensive paperbacks at discounted prices. Points earned for minimum orders are redeemable for prizes or free books.

Great Christian Books**, 229 South Bridge Street, P.O. Box 8000, Elkton, MD 21922–8000. (800) 775–5422. Books at a discount. Many home schooling titles are included. I order from them often, and love the selection and the prices. For a small membership fee of $5 a year, you will receive all their catalogs, and your membership is automatically renewed each time you order! Call or write for a catalog. If you are sponsored by a current member, you may be eligible to receive $3.00 off your order of $30.00 or more, and your friend will receive a $3.00 credit for sponsoring you!

Greenleaf Press, 1570 Old La Guardo Road, Lebanon, TN 37087. (615) 449–1617. (800) 331–1508. E-mail: GreenleafP @aol.com. Free catalog available. A home schooling family business run by Rob & Cyndy Shearer and their seven children. Although not a discount source, Greenleaf sells many unique items not found elsewhere and they publish, too. They specialize in "twaddle–free" living books for history. They also carry, *A School to Come Home to,* a fiction book for teens with a home schooler as a main character, written by Barbara Dunlop, a home school graduate. My daughter loves it. This book, and some of the art books carried by Greenleaf, sold me on them as a resource!

Home Education Press, P.O. Box 1083 Tonasket, WA 98855. (509) 486–1351. Home Education Press is best known for publishing *The Home Education Magazine.* They have also published other good books including an award–winning book of resource materials, *Good Stuff* by Rebecca Rupp. Back issues of their magazine are also available. The business is operated by Mark and Helen Hegener and their five home schooled children. Write to request their free catalog.

The Home School Books and Supplies, 104 S. West Ave., Arlington, WA 98223. (360) 435-0376. With over 100,000 titles and 450 publishers, the Jury family is bound to have what you are looking for. Their catalog is only a partial listing of what is available. Many items are discounted.

Home School Supply House, P.O. Box 7, Fountain Green, UT 84632. (800) 772-3129. Worth checking into for comparison prices. I was pleased to find "Family Math" for at least $2.00 less than I would pay anywhere else! They carry learning materials for all ages.

Homeschooling Book Club, 1000 E. Huron, Milford, MI 48381. (810) 685-8773. Differs from other book clubs in that there are no minimum purchase requirements, and they cater to home schoolers! Their Super-Saver discounts are really steep, so if you send a check or money order with your order, you can really save money!

John Holt's Book and Music Store, 2269 Massachusetts Avenue, Cambridge, MA 02140-1226. Many interesting books I haven't seen elsewhere. They also offer the *Growing Without Schooling* magazine.

Lifetime Books & Gifts, *The Always Incomplete Resource Guide & Catalog,* 3900 Chalet Suzanne Drive, Lake Wales, FL 33853-7763. (800) 377-0390. Send $3.00 for a huge and informative catalog. Bob and Tina Farewell have a very comprehensive stock of books on hand, including some out-of-print treasures. They carry some items for teaching challenged or special needs children.

Moore Foundation Catalog, Moore Foundation, Box 1, Camas, WA 98607. (360) 835-5500. Source for the Moore's books and other books they highly recommend. Not a discount source, but if you're looking for their excellent books, this is the place to order!

Rainbow Re–Source Center, Catalog of new, discounted, home schooling books and materials. Products my children enjoy are their blank books and decorated border sheets. Call or write for a free catalog. See their listing in the next section.

Scholastic Book Club, P.O. Box 7503, Jefferson City, MO 65102–9966. Catalogs published by grade–level range. Inexpensive paperbacks. Write to request catalogs for the grades you teach. Earn free books or gifts with points from your orders.

_____ (3b) Used curriculum materials _____

The Back Pack, P.O. Box 125, Ernul, NC 28527. (919) 637–5137. Run by home schooling couple, David and Joan Cowell, who sell new and used textbooks and home school–ing "helps." They also buy used textbooks. Write or call for a free catalogue.

Christian Curriculum Cellar, 4460 S. Carpenter Road, Modesto, CA 95358. (209) 538–3632. Kevin and Georgene Girouard buy and sell used textbooks, 25–75% off retail, depending upon the condition. Ask for a free catalog.

Follett Home Education, 5563 South Archer Avenue, Chicago, IL 60638–3098. (800) 554–5754. Follett sells used and older textbooks at discount prices. Over fifty publishers are represented including A Beka, Addison–Wesley, Bob Jones, Harcourt Brace, Modern Curriculum Press, and Zaner–Bloser. They offered Open Court math books for almost $2 less than what I paid another used curriculum dealer. Free catalog.

The Homeschool Seller, P.O. Box 19, Cherry Valley, MA 01611–3148. (508) 791–8332. E-mail: HSSeller@aol.com Honor system book and items listings for home schoolers. They run an ad and a 15% commission fee is paid only when the items sell. Run by Dave and Wendy Orth, home schooling parents of six. Write or call to request a free sample issue. $12.00 per year for 10 issues.

Little Schoolhouse, P.O. Box 88, Lawtey, FL 32058. (904) 782–1144. Cathy Bigsby sells new and used curriculum. She will sell used curriculum on consignment or give credit towards purchases. Write for her catalog of Christian materials.

Once Upon a Time Family Books, P.O. Box 296, Manchester, IA 52057. Our own family business, selling quality used books through the mail, specializing in classics, "books you loved as a child," and educational books. Also buy books through the mail. Send $1 for a list of over 1000 quality books!

Rainbow Re–source Center, P.O. Box 491, Kewanee, IL 61443–0491. (800) 705–8809 for voice mail and fax. Or (309) 937–3385. Subscriptions $12.00 for six issues. A business run by home schooling family Bob and Linda Schneider and children. (Also see the chapter on home businesses.) Used curriculum materials sold on consignment. The Schneiders also have a catalog of new home schooling materials sold at discount prices. Request a sample of the *Rainbow Re-Porter* (used materials) for $2.50.

Second Harvest, Rural Route 1, Box 75, Humphrey, NE 68642. (402) 923–1682. Used curriculum materials for 25–75% off retail. Owners Bob and Shelly Noonan. Write for a complete catalog of current books for $1.00.

___ (3c) Free and low-cost instructional materials ___

You can buy over-priced books and bimonthly magazines listing free offers from companies, but I have found these sources to be repetitive and rarely worth their price. Check them out at the library, or shuffle through one at a bookstore before you buy to see if it could actually pay for itself. Teacher's magazines often list "freebies" for teachers or class-rooms and many women's magazines will occasionally list free offers. Your home school magazines may also tell about current free offers from companies.

Following are sources of information on free or low-cost offers which might supplement your home schooling, or could be helpful to home school teachers. Items offered for a limited time are not listed here.

Christian Life Workshops, P.O. Box 2250, Gresham, OR 97030. (800) 225-5259. Call or write for their free *Suggested Reading List of Literature and History*, edited by Gregg Harris. If you ask, CLW will also send free information about the home schooling laws in your state. They also sell materials to help home schoolers.

Consumer Information Catalog, Consumer Information Center, P.O. Box 100, Pueblo, CO 81002. E-mail: cic.info@ pueblo.gsa.gov Send the message: SEND INFO Or Web http://www.gsa.gov/staff/pa/cic/cic.htm Catalog of free and low-cost US federal government publications of consumer interest. Topics of publications range from starting a small business to vegetarian diets. You or your children may want to order these pamphlets and booklets to incorporate into your schooling. I won't list specific offers from sources like this as they are often time limited. I don't want anyone to be disappointed with a rejection. Costs, even for postcard requests, can add up. Believe me, I know!

Homeschooling; The How to Newsletter, 10404 Huntsmoor Drive, Richmond, VA 23233. Free quarterly newsletter by Gayle Graham, author of the book *How To Home School: A Practical Approach.*

National Gallery of Art, Department of Education Resources, Education Division, 4th and Constitution Ave., N.W., Washington, DC 20565. Books, teaching packets, slides and videos available for loan. Ask for the National Gallery of Art Extension Program catalog.

The Relaxed Home Schooler, P.O. Box 2524, Cartersville, GA 30120. Free quarterly newsletter from Mary Hood, author of *The Relaxed Home School*.

Smithsonian Institution, Office of Elementary and Secondary Education, Arts & Industries Building, Room 1163/MRC 402, Washington DC 20560. Many free pamphlets, teacher's guides and booklets available, as well as guides, kits and videos for a fee. My children and I enjoyed the free Art to Zoo newsletters. Art to Zoo is a regular publication providing background information, lesson plans, and resource lists for teachers in science, social studies and art. Each issue focuses on a different topic. Write to request the free *Resource Guide for Teachers*. Additional guides are $5.00.

U.S. Geological Survey, Branch of Information Services, Box 25286, Denver Federal Center, MS 306, Denver, CO 80225. (800) 435-7627. Request a form for free non-technical publications on geology, hydrology, mapping, and related science topics. These pamphlets are great for supplementing your science curriculum. My son, the fledgling archaeologist, loved the big fossil poster for his room!

____ (3d) Computer software ____

Home Learning Software, P.O. Box 1948, Jamestown, NC 27282. Disks as low as $1.99. Great sounding shareware programs. HLS has separate categories for each subject. They have now also begun to carry commercial programs at

competitive prices. Send them a first class stamp for their
unique "CatalogOnADisk" or download it from their internet
site at http://members.aol.com/homelearn. There you will
also find information on the latest software for homeschooling and even a free program or two.

Kidtec, P.O. Box 5431, Auburn, CA 95604. Run by a home
schooling family of nine. Melanie and Tim Cornell screen
and discount the educational software they offer.

M&M Software, P.O. Box 15769, Long Beach, CA 90815–
0769. (800) 642–6163, for a free catalog. E-mail:
mmsoft@aol.com Sells disks with shareware, public domain
and freeware software. Shareware allows you to try the
software before paying additional fees to the author. Prices
range from $2.95 to $4.95, depending on the number of disks
ordered.

____ (3e) School supplies ____

*I haven't ordered items from all of these catalogs. I have, however,
reviewed them for educational quality and value. My concept of "wish
lists" is not meant to encourage a materialistic attitude. On the contrary,
my hope is that home schooling families will be able to see just how
much they can do on very little. When my children and I look at
catalogs and make a wish list, it is understood that we usually can't
afford those items at that price. However, I might find the same item or
a similar one at a garage sale or through bartering, and that possibility
brings the unattainable within reach! I don't have relatives eager to buy
my children gifts, but if you do, why not share some of your favorite
catalogs with those who truly don't know what to get the children for
gifts.*

Buck Hill Associates, P.O. Box 501, North Creek, NY 12853–
0501. Catalog of paper Americana including replicas of
reward posters, recruiting posters, handbills, etc. from 65¢ on

up. Good resource for history and social studies supplements.

Childcraft, 250 College Park, P.O. Box 1811, Peoria, IL 61656-1811. A colorful catalog, perfect for "wish lists." The company sells wood blocks, art easels and musical instruments as well as colorful and sturdy toys that are just plain fun! Prices seem high so I wouldn't request this catalog with the thought of saving money!

Essential Learning Products, 2300 West Fifth Avenue, P.O. Box 2590, Columbus, OH 43216-2590. Supplementary workbooks and materials for kindergarten through grade 8. You can get guided practice workbooks for as little as $3.50 each in math, writing, spelling, handwriting and more.

ESP Publishing, 7163 123rd Circle N., Largo, Florida 34643. (800) 643-0280. We used their Super Workbooks two years in a row. They are huge and work great for supplemental material but we ended up using less than half a workbook each year. I would have saved money by just ordering their *Jumbo Math Yearbook* at half the price, as the Math worksheets were used the most. The Super Workbooks seem expensive but if you have a student who loves workbook pages, check them out.

Happy Face School Supplies, Box 176A, RR 1, Petersburg, NY 12138. If you don't have access to a school supply store, this little catalog can fulfill your every want, from decorated pencils and animal-shaped erasers to stickers of all kinds. Reasonable prices.

KidsArt, P.O. Box 274, Mt. Shasta, CA 96067. Art teaching supplies and books. A good selection of fun and inspiring products. Includes fine art postcards, charcoal, paints, art paper, and books full of art projects. Fair prices.

Klutz Press, *Klutz Flying Apparatus Catalogue,* 2121 Staunton Ct., Palo Alto, CA 94306. (415) 424–0739. Http://www.klutz .com   Klutz Press books are wonderful. They are more than just books because they come with all the necessary materials to do whatever the book is about. The *Explorabook* comes with a magnifying glass, *The Incredible Claybook* comes with clay, the pages in *Board Games* are the boards to play various games on! What fun to learn and play while we read. Another good "wish list" catalog.

Lewis Publishing, Inc., P.O. Box 588, Rockford, IL 61105. (815) 964–7927. Low–cost posters and prints (50–cents and up), including 12 full–color art prints for $4.99. Other sets available. Use the posters for children's rooms or classrooms, or for studying art. Request a free catalog for educators.

School Zone Publishing Company, P.O. Box 777, Grand Haven, MI 49417. (800) 253–0564. You probably have seen these workbooks and flash cards in your local discount store, but the catalog has a more expansive selection including learning games and readers. Workbooks start at $2.25, flash cards at $2.59, and games run as low as $6.99. My children enjoy their money bingo which we found at a discount store for $5.00.

Timberdoodle Company, E. Spencer Lake Road, Shelton, WA 98584. For more than ten years Dan and Deb Deffin-baugh and their family have run the Timberdoodle business, specializing in hands–on learning products, particularly the German–made Fishertechnik building kits. Although discounted, prices still run high for many items. The catalog features math products, puzzles, drafting and electronic materials and even software. You will enjoy looking at the catalog and circling things for your ever–growing "wish list."

Tobin's Lab, 4312 W. Cactus Road, Suite 11, Glendale, AZ 85304. Hands–on science materials for families, from petri dishes to microscopes and binoculars. Some of the items are expensive [although most are under $10]. If you are only looking for some simple science materials, the prices are fair. Run by home schooling family, Mike and Tammy Duby.

Treetop Publishing, P.O. Box 085567, Racine, WI 53408–5567. (414) 884–0501. Publisher of "Bare Books," blank books for children's writing activities. Various sizes and designs. Prices start at $1.09 each. You may mix books of different sizes and include other items in the minimum order of 10 items. Catalog includes ideas for using Treetop products.

University Prints Catalogue, 21 East St., Winchester, MA 01890. 7500 basic art history prints listed by period, school, and artist. 5 ½ x 8 inch prints, 8¢ each for black and white prints and 18¢ each for the 300 color prints. Send $3 for a current catalogue.

4
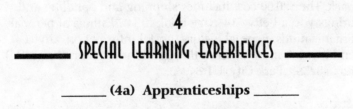
SPECIAL LEARNING EXPERIENCES

(4a) Apprenticeships

Ferguson's Guide to Apprenticeship Programs, Vol. 1 and 2, edited by C.J. Summerfield and Holli Cosgrove. J.G. Ferguson Publishing Co., Chicago, IL 1994. Listing of 1500 programs in 76 job categories that are currently available for apprenticeships. Also contains a state–by–state list of Bureau of Apprenticeship and Training offices.

Mentor Apprentice Exchange P.O. Box 405, Canning, Nova Scotia B0P 1H0, Canada. Published by Heidi Priesnitz, a long–time advocate of alternative learning. Her exchange newsletter provides practical information, articles, letters, ideas, ongoing support and unlimited free listings in the quarterly subscriber directory. Listings include both introductions by those seeking positions in the United States or Canada and available apprenticeships.

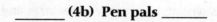

(4b) Pen pals

To find a pen pal, home schoolers may want to check listings in home schooling magazines such as Growing Without Schooling or Home Education Magazine. Women's Circle magazine also carries pen pal listings. For pen pals in other countries, try contacting one of these pen pal organizations: Kids Meeting Kids, Box 8H, 380 Riverside Drive, New York, NY 10025 (matches children aged 7-18 with pen pals), or Student Letter Exchange, 215 5th Ave SE Waseca, MN 56093. (For pen pals aged 10-21; send a SASE for an application form).

Making Mailbox Memories: *Global Pen Friends for Grownups and Kids* by Julia Anne Riley, Kindred Spirit Press, $20.00, paper-back. The $20.00 cost includes shipping and handling and brings you a hefty 314-page book full of listings of pen pal organizations, pen pal history, postal information, advice and ideas. Can be ordered through Kindred Spirit Press, P.O. Box 682560, Park City, UT 84068.

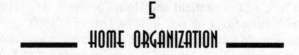

HOME ORGANIZATION

Emilie's Creative Home Organizer, by Emilie Barnes. Harvest House Publishers, 1995. My all-time favorite book on organization for homemakers. Every topic relating to home organization that you can think of and then some is covered. Hundreds of ideas and tips that will save you money, time and energy. Emilie Barnes is a nationally known home–management expert and speaker.

401 Ways to Get Your Kids to Work at Home by Bonnie R. McCullough and Susan W. Monson, 1981, St. Martin's Press, 175 5th Ave., New York, NY 10010. Techniques, tips and strategies on how to get your kids to share the housework. With nine children between them, these two women should know what works and what doesn't. Full of great ideas on organizing bedrooms, play areas, etc.

Get Your Act Together by Pam Young and Peggy Jones. Harper, 1993. A 7–day program for home management using 3x5 index cards. Great ideas on de–cluttering and organization but I winced when they advised throwing away all old magazines and newspapers. I would suggest filing particularly interesting or helpful articles before disposing of the magazines. I often use articles I've filed away for inspiration or reference. Another wonderful book by the same two sisters is *The Sidetracked Home Executives.*

How To Conquer Clutter by Stephanie Culp, Writer's Digest Books, 1989. Great ideas on home and office organization. Helpful hints that can easily be applied to home schooling organization.

Is There Life After Housework? by Don Aslett, Writer's Digest Books, 1992. From bookstores or call (800) 289–0963. Suggested retail price: $10.99. Don Aslett's approach to housework can save you time and frustration. This book shows the reader how to use professional cleaner's methods to really be efficient in your housework. Also by Don Aslett, and equally helpful; *Clutter's Last Stand, Clutter-free! Finally and Forever* and *Make Your House Do the Housework.*

G
HOME BUSINESS INFORMATION

Christian Home Business Journal, P.O. Box 402, Belgrade, MO 59714. $16 a year, 11 issues. Editor John Olwin and assistant editor Anne Olwin produce this newsletter to provide encouragement, help, and information for Christians in their home businesses.

Homemade Money — How to Select, Start, Manage, Market and Multiply the Profits of a Business at Home, 5th ed, by Barbara Brabec, Betterway Productions, 1994. P.O. Box 2137, Naperville, IL 60567-2137. Free brochure available. If there is only one book you read before starting up a home business, this should be it! Covers every conceivable subject related to home businesses. The book is available for $23.95 ppd. (Illinois residents add $1.34 sales tax).

Minding Your Own Business by Raymond and Dorothy Moore, Wolgemuth & Hyatt, 1990. Common sense guide to combining family and home business. Available from Moore Foundation, Box 1, Camas, WA 98607. (360) 835-2736.

The New Careers Center, 1515 23rd Street, Box 339-CT, Boulder, CO 80306. Whether your interest is in starting a home business, selling crafts, writing, or opening a small business, their *The Whole Work Catalog* probably contains a helpful book you can use. Write to request a free catalog.

Working From Home, 4th Edition, by Paul and Sarah Edwards. From Jeremy P. Tarcher/Putnam, 1994. All of the Edwards' book are very thorough and informative, and this one is no exception. The only complaint I have is their tendency to encourage child care during working hours. I think this defeats the purpose. I work at home so I can be with my children!

7
SAVING MONEY

_____ (7a) Books with ideas _____

Cheap Eating: *How to Feed Your Family Well And Spend Less* by Pat Edwards, Upper Access Books, 1993. $9.95 plus $3.00 shipping , P.O. Box 457, Hinesburg, VT 05461. (800) 356–9315. A good book with helpful ideas for saving money on your grocery bill.

Cut Your Spending in Half-Without Settling For Less by the editors of Rodale Press, Rodale Press, 1994. This book is subtitled *How to Pay the Lowest Price for Everything*, and that is just what it attempts to teach the reader. Tips and ideas on saving money at the supermarket, on home maintenance, appliances, furniture, decorating, real estate, cars, entertainment, children's expenses, and much more! Really thorough in covering all the bases.

Dinner's in the Freezer! *More Mary and Less Martha* by Jill Bond. 1993, 3rd edition, $20 from Great Christian Books, P.O. Box 254, Elkton, MD 21922–0254. Jill shows readers how to manage their household in an orderly manner. Her book includes information on her unique system for cooking and freezing meals for six months at a time. Tempting recipes are included in almost every chapter. I loved Jill's book. She made me believe I, too, could become more of a "Mary" in my household!

Eat Well for $50 a Week, by Rhonda Barfield, Lilac Publishing, P.O. Box 665, St. Charles, MO 63302–0665. $12.95 (includes shipping). This book covers the many ways a family can save money on groceries. These include warehouse shopping, bulk–buying, couponing, and excellent, simple recipes her family uses. Rhonda really feeds her family of five on $50.00 a week and inspires the reader to duplicate her feat! Her new book, *15-Minute Cooking*, will be a boon to the home schooling mom who feels like a short-order cook. With 100 recipes and step-by-step instructions, Rhonda shows how family cooking can be accomplished in two 15-minute time periods each day.

The Heart Has Its Own Reasons by Mary Ann Cahill, LaLeche League International, 1983. Check out used bookstores or your library for this one as it is no longer in print! My copy is falling apart as it has been read so many times at 2:00 a.m. while nursing and rocking a baby. If you need a reason to stay home with your young children, read this! If you need a *way* to make it financially feasible to do so, this book is for you! Hints, thoughts, and ideas from mothers at home.

Homeschooler's Save-a-penny Press 12056 Mt. Vernon Ave., Suite 182, (909) 872-1128. A classified ad newspaper published 8 times each year. Ads are mostly from individuals selling their used curriculum materials.

How to Raise a Family & a Career Under One Roof by Lisa M. Roberts. To be published by Bookhaven Press, 401 Amherst Ave., Moon Township, PA 15108. $14.95. Examination of the prepublication proof sheets of this book indicate that it will be well written and meaningful. The topic is of interest for home school parents. Practical, emotional, and spiritual values are discussed.

Miserly Moms: *Living on One Income in a Two-Income Economy*, Second Edition by Jonni McCoy. Order through GCB Publishing (410) 392-3590. Helpful tips, hints, and ideas from a mother who left the work force to stay home with her children and learned to live on half of their income. Help to buy groceries on $40 per week

More-With-Less Cookbook by Doris Janzen Longacre, Herald Press, 1976. Mennonite recipes and suggestions for cooking well on less money. Advice we can all use.

1,001 Bright Ideas to Stretch Your Dollars, 1995, $10.99, from Servant Publications. Author Cynthia Yates covers food preparation, hospitality, gift giving, home care, home decorating, automobiles, and more. And she numbered her ideas up to 1,001. "Our home is small. And it is not fancy. Yet we welcome people through in shifts!. . . . It even shouts, 'Howdy, partner, pull up a chair and sit a spell!'. . . . If you are discouraged because decorating dollars don't even qualify for a slot on your budget, then buck up, Buckaroo! This chapter is for you!"

1,001 Ways to Cut Your Expenses by Jonathan D. Pond, Dell Publishing, 1992. 666 Fifth Ave., New York, NY 10103. This book is about living beneath your means and spending less money than you earn. Easy reading and simple ideas with good points you may not have thought of.

Saving Money Any Way You Can: *How to Become a Frugal Family*, by Mike Yorkey, 1994, Servant Publications, P.O. Box 8617, Ann Arbor, MI 48107. A great book with wonderful ideas, but as a self-proclaimed coupon queen, I'd have to correct some misconceptions about coupon use that Yorkey inaccurately portrays. For instance, you can't use two coupons on two items if you are using a buy-one-get-one-free store coupon. You can only use a coupon on the item you are buying, not the one you get free. Some of his gener-alizations (*you can't find clothes for children past age six at garage sales*) are simply untrue for those of us who are used to scrimping and saving. I found myself wishing that Lou Gage, the real-life "super-saver" he quotes and uses as an example would write a book! Yorkey's book is chock-full of great ideas, so it is a worthwhile read.

Tightwad Gazette and **Tightwad Gazette II** by Amy Dacyczyn, Villard Books, 1993 and 1995, respectively. Here is a woman who practices what she preaches. Even now, with two books and a thriving newsletter on the market, she lives simply, buying her family's wardrobe at garage sales and making homemade inexpensive breakfasts. A self–described "frugal zealot", Amy has added her ideas to hundreds compiled from her subscribers. Her two books are very helpful whether you are looking for ways to save on the necessities, or only want some creative ideas for Halloween costumes.

_____ (7b) Newsletters _____

The editors of some newsletters designed for "tightwads," "cheapskates," or "frugal consumers" now make a living by sharing their ideas and their reader's ideas in the public forum, whether it is their monthly newsletters or the many books now being written on the subject. Most talk shows have hosted one of these editors and supermarket tabloids have featured a tightwad story. The talk shows and the tabloids center in on one or two oddities of these women like hanging cloth diapers in the attic during the winter; rinsing out and re-using sealable plastic bags; or clothing the entire family through secondhand finds. What isn't sensational enough to be big news is how so many families live on one income – how they actually thrive on less. You don't have to rinse out your sandwich bags and make statues from your dryer lint to save money. But you can learn from the experiences of those who are making ends meet. That is what these newsletters and books can do for you.

Cheapskate Monthly, P.O. Box 2135, Paramount, CA 90723–8135. E–mail: cheapsk8@ix.netcom.com Internet: http://www.cheapsk8.com   A newsletter from Mary Hunt, $15.95 a year. Two paperback books available through the same address, published by St. Martin's Press, $4.50 each :*The Best of Cheapskate Monthly, Simple Tips for Living Lean in the '90's* and *The Cheapskate Monthly Money Makeover*. Recipes, reader tips, hints, and ideas on saving money and living within one's means.

Christian Home Swapletter, P.O. Box 107, Mechanicstown OH 44651-0107. Published by Laurie Colecchi. You may have a sample for $1.00 and a stamp. A $16.00 yearly subscription fee entitles the subscriber unlimited free advertising for items they have to swap. Whether clothing or curriculum materials, barter trades are an inexpensive way to acquire needed items.

Frugal Times ... Making-Do With Dignity, P.O. Box 5877, Garden Grove, CA 92645. (714) 891-3792. Tracey McBride edits this lovely little newsletter which is designed "to promote the single-mindedness and goal setting needed to get our lives in order while being frugal." With regular features such as *Frugal Luxuries, Creative Recycling of the Ordinary,* and *Home-keeping,* Tracey brings a creative energy to a subject that can appear overdone or become stale in similar newsletters. $12.00 a year for eight issues.

Home School Exchange 26 Colony St., St. Augustine, FL 32095. $.6.50/yr. US$9.50 to Canada. A classified ad newspaper for home educators. Bi-monthly. (800) 894-8247; Fax (904) 824-8247.

No-Debt Living Newsletter, P.O. Box 282, Veradale, WA 99037. $25 a year, 11 issues. Editor Robert E. Frank approaches financial management and investment strategies from a Christian viewpoint. This newsletter encourages living without debt. It helps its readers get control of their finances and use their resources wisely.

Refund Express, P.O. Box 179, Commerce, GA 30529. Single issue $3, for 12 months $26. Editor: Sandy Ennis. A refunder's bonanza, listing current money-back offers, free premiums, and all the current refund offers. Chock-full of reader's letters, articles, tips, and ideas for increasing your refunding potential. Also includes classifieds for refunding and coupon trading. Sandy makes refunding *fun*.

Refunding Makes Cents, Box 969, Bountiful, UT 84011. Sample $2.95, 1 Year $25. In this newsletter you will find informative articles, lists of current refund offers, and classified ads from readers. Editor Michele Easter has also written a book, *Shop Like a Coupon Queen*, available for $3.99 plus $1.25 postage/handling at the same address. I highly recommend it to anyone interested in getting more involved in couponing or refunding.

Simple Living News, P.O. Box 1884, Jonesboro, GA 30237-1884. E-mail: KiLgo@MindSpring.com The goal of this newsletter is to encourage those searching for a lifestyle with less stress, more time with family, and a "saner lifestyle that generates more peace and personal fulfillment." Published and edited by Edith Flowers Kilgo, One year (10 issues) $16.

Index

Index